BASICS OF AMERICAN LABOUR LAW

Second Version 2022

Antoine T.J.M. Jacobs

OPEN PRESS TiU

Basics of American Labour Law

A Brief Description of the Labour Law of the United States of America for the Purpose of Comparative Labour Law (Second version 2022)

Author: Prof. dr. Antoine T.J.M. Jacobs

ISBN: 9789403673936
DOI: 10.26116/2b6d-c664

Published by: Open Press TiU
Contact details: info@openpresstiu.edu
https://www.openpresstiu.org/

Cover Design by: Kaftwerk, Janine Hendriks
Layout Design by: Wolf Publishers, Claudia Tofan

Open Press TiU is the academic Open Access publishing house for Tilburg University and beyond. As part of the Open Science Action Plan of Tilburg University, Open Press TiU aims to accelerate Open Access in scholarly book publishing.

Table of Contents

Abbreviations

ADA	Americans with Disabilities Act
ADEA	Age Discrimination in Employment Act
EEOC	Equal Employment Opportunity Commission
EPA	Equal Pay Act
EU	European Union
FLSA	Fair Labour Standards Act
FMCS	Federal Mediation and Conciliation Service
FMLA	Family and Medical Leave Act
ILO	International Labour Organisation
LGBTQ	Lesbian, Gay, etc.
LL	Labour Law
LMRA	Labour Management Relations Act
LMRDA	Labour-Management Reporting and Disclosure Act
NLRA	National Labour Relation Act
NLRB	National Labour Relations Board
OSHA	Occupational Safety and Health Act
SSL	Social Security Law
US(A)	United States (of America)
UK	United Kingdom
WARNWorker	Adjustment and Retraining Notification Act

CHAPTER I

Introduction

The United States of America is a genuine federal state, formed by 50 States on the American continent under the umbrella of a Federal government.[1] It is much more a federal state than the European Union. The federal authorities have more power to make all-American politics and all-American laws than authorities in Europe possess to produce all-European policies and laws, and where national states still have more political and legal autonomy than has been left for the States of the USA.

Labour Law is certainly one of the fields where this difference is quite noticeable.

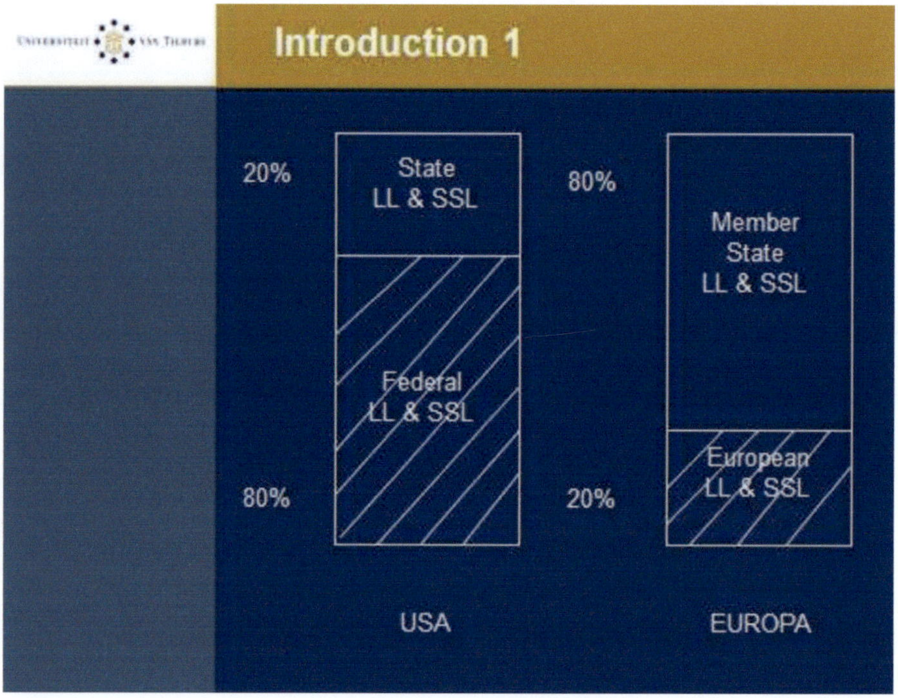

If I had to assess the impact of federal labour law on the American labour market, I would come at 80%; in Europe the impact of EU labour law I would estimate it at 20%. This would leave the impact of State law on the American labour market at 20%, while in Europe the impact of national labour law on their labour markets would be 80%. Of course, this is not more than an assessment at random, but I believe that most labour market experts will join this assessment.

Obviously, this cohabitation of federal labour law with the law of the States will cause legal and practical difficulties (see par. 1.1.2.)

1. IEL § 8.

A lot of students will raise other questions. Why is American labour law as it is – often so different from the law in other states? And can we expect in the nearby future changes in the present state of American Labour Law?

For an answer on these questions, we have to understand the background of labour law, and have some idea of the size, geographical situation, population, culture, economic data etc. of the USA. One can find such information at numerous places.[2]

To understand actual US labour law and the possibilities for changes in USA labour law I want to focus your attention on the constitutional and the political situation in the USA.

1.1. The Constitutional/Political situation

1.1.1. The Constitutional situation

In the USA statutory labour law is generated at two levels, the Federal and the State level.

Federal labour law[3]

Federal labour law, laid down in federal Acts, is produced by Congress, which consists of two chambers, the Senate (100 members) and the House of Representatives (circa 435 members) and must be signed by the President of the USA (who therefore has a limited right to veto).

The President of the USA also has the power to make labour law by issuing Executive Orders for the Federal Administration. He does this frequently in the field of labour law for the federal public services (ca. 75.000 workers) and for contractors doing business with the Federal authorities (ca. 300.000 workers).

American law is administered by a large bureaucracy whose staff, structures and procedures have a very real impact on the nature of that law.[4] For labour law at federal level there are various Boards and Authorities, established by federal acts to implement and interpret federal legislation, notably in the field of labour-management relations, anti-discrimination law and health and safety.

Finally, federal labour law is interpreted and adjudicated by the Federal Courts, in last instance the Supreme Court of the USA.

2. IEL §§ 1-7; Jacobs.
3. IEL §§ 8-16.
4. IEL § 107; Jacobs § 11.5.

State labour law[5]

State labour law, laid down in State Acts, is produced by the Legislature/ Assembly of the State, which consists of two chambers[6], the Senate and the House of Representatives of the State and must be signed by the Governor of the State (who therefore has a limited right to veto).

The Governor of the State also has the power to make labour law by issuing Executive Orders. He does this frequently in the field of labour law for the State public services and for contractors doing business with the State authorities.

Also at State level a lot of law is produced by the various Boards and Authorities, established by State Acts to implement and interpret State Legislation. For State labour law this is e.g. true in areas of anti-discrimination law.

Finally, State labour law is adjudicated and interpreted by the State Courts, in last instance the Supreme Court of the State.[7] However, also the U.S. Supreme Court can reject a state law that violates the U.S. Constitution.

1.1.2. The Political situation[8]

There are two main forces in American politics, the Republicans, who in general do not like expansion of statutory labour law, and the Democrats, who in general are in favour of improvements of existing statutory labour law. These two forces are omnipresent in the USA, at Federal level and at the level of the States.

In various States, notably in the North-East and on the Pacific Coast, Democrats usually have the majority, in other States, especially in the Mid-West, Republicans usually have the majority, while in several States, e.g. Florida, the majority easily swings from Democrats to Republicans and v.v.

At federal level, the majority may swing at every election (there are elections every 2 years for a (partly) renewal of the houses of Congress and every 4 years for the USA Presidency).

5. IEL p. 8-16.
6. Only the legislature of Nebraska is unicameral. It consists solely of the state senate.
7. Only in the state of New York it is called: the Court of Appeal.
8. IEL §§ 20-24; Jacobs § 1.4.

The federal level concerning the US Presidency in recent years have seen:

1981 - 1993 Republicans (Reagan/W. Bush)

1993 – 2001 Democrat (Clinton)

2001 – 2009 Republican (G.W. Bush)

2009 – 2017 Democrat (Obama)

2017 – 2021 Republican (Trump)

2021 - ...... Democrat (Biden)

Congress has seen majorities, sometimes similar to that of the US Presidency, often also unlike the US Presidency.

The years of	Clinton				Bush				Obama				Trump		Biden
	92	94	96	98	*00*	*02*	*04*	*06*	08	10	12	14	*16*	*18*	20
President	D		D		*R*		*R*		D		D		*R*		D
Senate	D	D	*R*	*R*	D	*R*	*R*	D	D	D	D	*R*	*R*	*R*	D
House	D	*R*	*R*	*R*	*R*	*R*	*R*	D	D	*R*	*R*	*R*	*R*	D	D

As for issuing a federal statute a majority in both the Senate and the House of Representatives + the endorsement of the President is needed, changes in the law are only easily possible if these three institutions at the same time are in the same Democratic or Republican hands. Even then it is possible for the opposition to block the adoption of bills by using the tactics of the filibuster) (minimum 40 members in the Senate).[9] To go around this hurdle an Act must be framed through the budget reconciliation legislative process which would require a bare-minimum 50-vote majority plus a tie-breaking vote of the Vice-President who is a party-member of the President, so actually a Democrat.

In earlier decades it usual happened that – when there were different majorities in the three institutions - compromises were forged by a Democrat Congressman and a Republican Congressman – that is why so many Acts are named after the two “sponsors”. Nowadays such compromise Acts have become very difficult because of the antagonism between Democrats and Republicans.

9. See on ‘filibuster’ IEL § 805.

The President may veto any Statute adopted by Congress that he does not like, but Congress may override such a veto.

As the President alone may issue Executive Orders for the various parts of the Federal Administration, in recent years Presidents have often laid down in Executive Orders certain labour standards for which they had no majority in Congress. In such a way those norms were rolled out in the federal Civil Service and imposed on private contractors which want to do business with the Government. If often happened that an incoming President nullified orders made by his predecessor of a different political colour. Trump did this already with several labour law Orders of Obama. And Biden did the same with Trumps' Executive Orders.

All Statutes and all Executive Orders of the President can be quashed by the federal courts, when they can be seen as contrary to the American Constitution, in latest instance by the Supreme Court of the US.

This Court has only 9 Members, nominated for lifetime by the President of the USA with the consent of the Senate. It is usual that the President nominates his political friends. Since many years, this Court has had a shaky balance between pro-Republican and pro-Democrat judges, nominated by the Republican resp. Democrat Presidents. As Trump could nominate 3 new judges the actual composition of the USA Supreme Court is in favour of the Republicans.

(center) left Nominated by Democrat Presidents	(center) right Nominated by Republican Presidents
	Roberts
Breyer	Thomas
Sotomayor	Alito
Kagan	Gorsuch
	Kavanaugh
	Barrett

Also, the nominations of lower federal judges and the Board members of the federal agencies, which must often have the approval of US Senate, are very much politicized. For Labour Law this is extremely important for the National Labour Relations Board.[10]

This entire party-political game is also played at the government of the various States.

10. IEL § 805.

1.2. The Hierarchy in Labour Law

1.2.1. Interstate commerce

One of the typical characteristics of American law in general, so also of American Labour law, is that the Federation has not always full competence to issue laws. Over the years this competence has been heavily contested. One of the legal bases for the Federation is, that it is, according to the U.S. Constitution, competent to issue laws about 'interstate commerce'. This is now a recognised legal basis for the adoption of Federal labour law. However, at the same time this implies, that often, federal Labour laws offer no complete coverage on the American labour market. Companies which lack the ambition to engage in interstate commerce, for instance a village tobacco shop, are not within the scope of such important Acts as the FLSA (see par. 2.7.) and the NLRA (see par. 3.1.1.).

1.2.2. Pre-emption

The Supremacy Clause in the federal Constitution gives federal Law priority over State Law. Any conflicts between federal and State law must be resolved in favour of federal law. And even if there is not a direct conflict with federal law, State law must give way if federal law is designed to be the exclusive body governing an area of regulation that is within the federal government's constitutional competence.[11] This is the famous doctrine of Pre-emption. This means that in all areas in which there is Federal Labour Law there is priority of this Federal Law over State Law. However, in many areas the States may supplement or even deviate from Federal law. But this is very complicated doctrine.

1.2.3. The impact of the Constitution and of International treaties[12]

We have already seen that the Constitution of the USA has a certain impact on the division of powers between the federal authorities and the States, also in labour law. It has also consequences for the contents of labour law – labour laws of the federation cannot violate the USA Constitution and State labour Laws cannot violate the State Constitutions. If they do, the Supreme Court of the USA or the Supreme of the State will quash them.

This force of Constitutions occasionally may benefit the individual worker, certainly the civil servants.

11. IEL § 825.
12. Jacobs § 1.6.

The labour law standards contained in international treaties do not have much impact on the American worker, although in theory treaties which have been ratified can have binding effect. However, the USA has not ratified many international treaties that contain labour standards and of the few that the USA has ratified, the courts have only very seldom recognised binding effect on the parties of the employment contracts.

Sometimes the Legislature of US states by way of a resolution may pronounce that it recognises supports and implements the principle of a certain treaty.[13]

An important Treaty for Labour Law has been the North Atlantic Free Trade Agreement (NAFTA) between the USA, Canada and Mexico, concluded by the Democratic Clinton Administration in 1996. This Treaty has often been compared with the EU Treaty, but it had much more limited ambition. It was about free movement of goods, services and capital, but not about free movement of persons/workers. Nevertheless, it was always under criticism of the Republicans and the Trump Administration abolished it, replacing it by the United States-Mexico-Canada Agreement (USMCA), creating a more balanced, reciprocal trade agreement. This actual agreement quite remarkably has pushed the Mexicans to establish real trade union freedom in their country! The Biden Administration has not abolished USMCA but wants to develop further its potentials.

1.3. Enforcement

For resolving Labour Law disputes the USA does not have one clear system of labour law courts as in many EU countries. The adjudication of labour cases is fragmented in a variety of tribunals, with four major tribunals, each dominating an area of substantive law:[14]

First, *state courts* deal primarily with individual contracts, applying both federal and state labour laws as well as the common civil law; they also have as a secondary responsibility the reviewing of administrative decisions of state agencies, mentioned under third;

Second, *federal courts* – the federal district courts, the Courts of Appeal and the US Supreme Court – have as their primary responsibility the enforcing of federal labour laws, and as their secondary responsibility the reviewing of administrative decisions of the federal agencies, mentioned under third;

13. See for instance Californian Senate Concurrent Resolution No. 78 Chapter 16 (2018) on the Convention on the Elimination of All Forms of Discrimination against Woman.

14. Jacobs § 11.2.

Third, *agencies* that provide first instance judgments, such as the National Labour Relations Board and the Equal Employment Opportunity Commission at Federal level and – at State level – e.g. the State Labour Commissioner in California.

Fourth, *labour arbitrators* are often adjudicating disputes between unions and employers as to the meaning and application of collective agreements. Most collective agreements have an arbitration provision, that normally specifies that unresolved disputes regarding the agreement shall be decided by arbitration. Nevertheless, some collective agreements do not have such an agreement and some agreements expressly exclude certain categories of disputes from the arbitration provision. Not only are arbitration awards the governing law in the specific cases, but labour arbitration decisions often are published and form a body of persuasive precedent that guides future decisions by being treated as "the common law of the shop".[15]

Moreover, arbitration is not only used in disputes about collective agreements. It may also apply in cases between workers and employers in case their employment contract provided for such an agreement. Such agreements, in principle, would prevent employees to bring their employment disputes to the court. This result is nowadays increasingly contested. Sometimes the Federal legislator has intervened, like, recently, in cases of workplace sexual harassment or assaults.[16]

1.4. Applicable State Law

Considering the many varieties in the labour law between the US states, important are the rules on the applicable law of contract inside the US. Is on a worker, living and working in California in the service of a company based in New York the law of New York or the law of California applicable? The relevant rules can be learned from the Restatement of the Conflict of Laws, 2d. Exceptions apart they read:

> *The first rule is that courts will abide by a contractual choice of law made by the parties to a contract of employment, unless rules of that chosen state violates a strong public policy of the state in which the contract is being enforced.*
>
> *The second rule is that in the absence of a choice of law provision in the contract of employment American courts apply the 'most significant relationship' approach which will normally point to the law of the State were the contract of employment is executed.*[17]

15. IEL §§ 117/718-724.
16. The Ending Forced Arbitration of Sexual Assault and Sexual Harassment Act of 2021.
17. IEL §§ 974-975; Jacobs § 11.11.

1.5. No uniform labour law[18]

It may be clear from the foregoing observations, that US labour law is far from uniform. There is Federal and State Labour Law. However, there is the statutory law that covers most workers, but there is also special statutory law for special categories of workers, like civil servants (there are laws for the federal civil servants and each State has its own laws for the civil servants of the state)[19], seafarers[20], the railways, the mining industry, etc.

Then there is the law of the collective agreements, very important for those who are covered by it (see par. 2.3.), but as we shall further see (in par. 3.3.1.), only few American workers are covered by collective agreements. In the private sector only 7%.

For the 93% of the American employees in the private sector who are not working under collective agreements, there is, besides the statutory law, only the judge-made common law (see par. 2.1.) available to regulate their relationship with management.

Finally, there is the big divide between workers (93% of the American labour market) and independent contractors (7% of the American labour market). Those independent contractors are covered by very few statutory labour laws and not by collective agreements. For them there remains the common law of contract of services to regulate their business with their counterparts.

18. IEL § 108; Jacobs § 1.5.

19. IEL §§ 190-203.

20. IEL §§ 187-218.

CHAPTER II

Individual Labour Law

2.1. Introduction

Traditionally courts in the USA have solved all problems arising out of the individual contract of employment on the basis of the common law like in the UK. There has never been a codification of the law on the contract of employment like in France, The Netherlands, etc. In the course of time the roll of the common law has declined as increasingly more statutory federal and State law has been created, touching the contract of employment. However, as there has never been a complete codification of the law on the contract of employment in the US, the common law still plays its role on all questions not touched by State or federal Labour Law. See for instance on the issue's liability for mistakes by the workers (par. 2.13) and non-compete agreements (see par. 2.17)

This common law of employment is by way of case law made in the courts of the various States. Therefore, it may differ from one State to another. However, there is much similarity as the courts in the various States tend to look to each other. Scholars and lawyers have made USA-wide compilations of this common law, often called "Restatements of the law" issued by the American Law Institute. These are in principle unbinding compilations, but they exercise a great influence on the more or less "unpolitical" aspects of the law on the contract of employment.[1]

The most important Federal laws regarding the individual aspects of the contract of employment are:

- Fair Labour Standards Act 1938
- Equal Pay Act 1963
- Anti-Discrimination Laws 1964/1967/1991
- Family and Medical Leave Act 1993
- Occupational Safety and Health Act 1970
- Plant Closing Act (WARN-Act) 1988
- Davis-Bacon Act and similar Acts 1931/1965

Examples of State Laws regarding the individual aspects of the contract of employment can often be found in:

- Anti-Discrimination laws, notably in the field of affirmative action and sexual orientation
- Wage payment statutes
- State Minimum Wages Acts

1. For Employment Law see the most recent issues of the Restatement (Second) of Contracts and the Restatement of Employment Law.

- Working Hours Acts
- Acts on non-compete agreements
- Acts against abuses in temporary agencies work

2.2. The contract of employment

In the USA there is no uniform definition of the contract of employment. Acts of the Federation and of the various States have their own definitions in order to define more precisely the scope of those statues.[2] However there is much concordance in the definitions. Also, the courts in defining whether a contract is a contract of employment or not - in principle do agree. A good example of all this may be the definition of "employee" in a State law of New Jersey: employee means any individual who performs services for and under the control and direction of an employer for wages or other remuneration."[3] This may lead us to the conclusion that in the USA like in Europe, the basic elements of the definition of employment are work, pay and subordination (= under the control and direction of an employer).

This definition, like in Europe, in theory makes it possible to distinguish the contract of employment from the work of self-employed, *independent contractors*. The traditional test has been, also like in Europe, the so-called control test. The essence of the contract of employment is, that the worker was subject to the command of the master as to the way in which he shall do his work. It is the right of control, not actual control that is important.[4]

In 1946 the US Supreme Court patented a new test[5]: a self-employed person is characterised by a number of features – he or she owns the assets, runs the risk of losses, is not obliged to do the work personally, etc. The test works negatively: Where the subject is not self-employed according to the test, he or she is regarded as an employee.

For this test of self-employment, the American courts are often using par. 220 of the Restatement (Second) of Agency, which refers to 10 elements to check.[6] Official services are often using a list of 20 factors, drawn up by the tax authorities (Internal Revenue Service).

---

2. IEL § 52; Jacobs § 8.9.
3. See s 34:19-2 of the New Jersey Conscious Employee Protection Act.
4. IEL § 119-123; Jacobs § 8.10.
5. (1946) 331 US 705 (US v Silk).
6. IEL § 125.

There is also a special provision in the Californian Labour Code (art. 3357), creating a legal assumption. Any person rendering service for another, other than as an independent contractor, or unless expressly excluded herein, is presumed to be an employee.

However, new economic and technological developments are constantly challenging the various aspects of these tests. So, for example in California the "gig economy" caused the Cal. Supreme Court[7] and then the legislators[8] to further toughen the criteria so-that possibly more "gig" workers, e.g. Uber drivers, may be classified as employees and so enjoy the protection of several state labour laws, like minimum wage, overtime pay, unemployment benefits, paid leaves, health insurance, right to unionise etc. The California AB5 Act limits "contract work" to "(A) jobs free from control or direction of the hiring entity in connection of the performance of the work" (B) "jobs performed outside the normal scope of the hiring entity's business" and (C) jobs "in which the worker is routinely doing work in an independently established trade, occupation or profession of the same nature of the work performed." This Act of the Democratic Legislature of California has been hailed by unions, but detested by Republicans and other people, who claim that this Act has disrupted the livelihood of freelancers and gig economy workers across the State. By a referendum in 2020 California voters approved Proposition 22, which stripped out the main provision of the AB5 Act, covering rideshare drivers (Uber).

At federal level the Trump Administration has tried to help the gig-companies and other employers by issuing, in 2020, the Independent Contractor Rule. This rule weighs multiple factors when considering whether a worker is an employee or independent contractor, but places greater weight on the person's control over the work and the person's opportunity for profit or loss. In May 2021, this rule was rescinded by the Biden Administration but not replaced with a new interpretation. The Biden Administration restored the long-standing multi-factor test established since 2008 by judicial precedent, which outlined a seven factor "economic realities" test. However, a Texas court decided in 2022 that the Biden administration failed to properly seek public input when it cancelled the rule, putting the Trump standard back on the books. Then the Biden administration announced it would start another rulemaking process.

---

7. (2018) Cal. Sup. Ct. April 30, 2018 (Dynamex Operations); California Labour Commissioner, June 3 2015, Case nr. 11-46739, Super Ct. Case No. CGC-15-546378 Uber Techs Inc. v. Berwick).

8. California Assembly Bill 5 ("Gig "Economy Rights Bill" or "AB5"), September 12, 2019.

There is a tricky dichotomy for the Biden administration: how do you maintain independent contractor relationship for workers who enjoy that freedom, while also ensuring workers aren't being exploited under that model?

In the meantime, the US House of Representatives has already approved the so-called Protecting the Right to Organise Act (PRO Act) (see par. 3.3.1) which will bring a California-like definition in the NLRA, and other federal labour laws.

In the US there is no consensus about the legal status of Temporary Agency Work.[9] The employer of such a temporary agency worker may be the temporary work agency or the user. Also, a joint employer-ship may be assumed.[10] This situation may lead to abuses (see 2.24.).

2.3. The impact of the Collective Agreement

As has been said before, there are not many American workers under a collective agreement, only 7% in private industry. However, for these American employees covered by a collective agreement, this is a prime source of rights and obligations. Collective agreements are in the USA regarded as legally enforceable contracts.[11] The case law of the US Supreme Court has established that the contents of a collective agreement become part of the contract of employment of *all* employees of the workforce within the scope of a collective agreement (whether unionised or not) of an employer that is bound to a collective agreement.

In Europe the collective agreement almost always gives the minimum conditions of employment of the employees subject to it. The employer cannot deviate from the collective agreement *in peius* (to the disadvantage of the worker), but he can deviate *in melius* (when it is more favourable to the employee). In the US however the collective agreement is seldom regarded as a minimum. It is generally seen as a standard from which the employer cannot deviate even if it is *in melius*. Unions might see a deviation of the collective agreement *in melius* an unfair labour practice – the employer is able to grant the employees more rights and benefits that the unions could have extorted from him by concluding the collective agreement! At the same time, this legal situation is a trap for the unions, because it often plays into the cards of the employer: he may discourage

9. D. Jamieson, California enacts Landmark Law for Temp Workers, Huffington Post, September 2014, retrieved from https:www.huffingtonpost.com/2014/09/20/California temp workers Ln 5901142.html

10. IEL § 126; Jacobs § 8.6.

11. IEL § 116.

his employees not to join a trade union because then he is able to offer them better working conditions.[12]

For those employees covered by a collective agreement, there is a second embarrassing point. Those workers are not supposed to go to court to invoke the conditions of their contracts of employment. Usually, it is the union representative who takes the action for them invoking the collective agreement. They pursue all claims through the so-called grievances/arbitration procedures, which is provided for in the relevant collective agreement (see 3.3.7).[13]

2.4. The impact of company handbooks

For the vast majority of American employees (90%), not covered by collective agreements, there may exist so-called company handbooks/ employee handbooks/manuals/staff-guides. Notably employers of the greater companies are using these handbooks to provide a consistent set of policies and procedures. And also to implement the many laws which require employers to notify their employees of certain workplace rights. The company handbooks are most of the time unilaterally established by the employers. When hired, employees typically are told they should be familiar with and are required to sign a receipt for the handbook.

There are no federal or state laws requiring employers to have a company handbook and plenty employers choose not to have one. And the employers, who opted to have one, often have inserted "disclaimers" in these documents in order to avoid legal claims based on handbook texts that surpass the statutory obligations of the employer. The binding force of a company handbook depends very much on the text of the handbooks and an eventually disclaimer. As the common law in the various States of the USA is not uniform, there is no single approach of the courts about the binding force of these documents. It only can be said that most courts decline to enforce an employee handbook provision if the document contains a clear prominently displayed disclaimer announcing that the policies contained in the book do not constitute a contractual commitment.[14]

2.5. Discrimination

The American federal statutory rules against discrimination at work date back to the 1870s, when they were issued as § 1870 and § 1871 of an act, that

12. Jacobs § 9.5.

13. IEL §§ 59/828-829.

14. IEL § 148; Jacobs § 9.2.

is now still on the statute book as 42 US Code §§ 1981 and 1983.[15] Although these provisions can still be useful for the fight against discrimination at work, most attention is now focussed on four great modern Federal Laws against discrimination.[16]

1) The 1963 Equal Pay m/f Act, see par 2.8.
2) The 1964 Civil Rights Act, and especially its Title VII, which makes it an unfair employment practice to discriminate because of race, colour, religion, sex or national origin.[17]

The Act is only applicable on companies with 15 or more employees whose business affects interstate commerce (see par. 2.1.1). The Act prohibits racial discrimination, as well as discrimination on national origin.[18] It outlaws religious discrimination[19] and finally it forbids sex discrimination.[20] This last notion includes pregnancy discrimination[21] and sexual harassment,[22] but is does not explicitly prohibit discrimination on the basis of sexual orientation.[23]

3) the 1967 Age Discrimination in Employment Act (ADEA) offers Americans over 40 years protection against age discrimination in employment.[24]

The Act is only applicable on companies with 20 or more.

4) the 1990 Americans with Disabilities Act (ADA)[25] protects from on-the-job discrimination individuals who have a physical or mental impairment that substantially limits any major life activity. It entitles the disabled worker to "reasonable accommodation" of his working environment (but an accommodation that would pose an undue hardship on an employer is not a "reasonable" accommodation and needs not to be provided).

The Act is only applicable on companies with 15 or more employees.

15. IEL §§ 308-317.
16. Jacobs § 7.1.
17. IEL §§ 318-320.
18. IEL § 341; Jacobs § 7.5.
19. IEL § 342; Jacobs § 7.6.
20. Jacobs § 7.7.
21. IEL §§ 334-335.
22. IEL §§ 336-339.
23. IEL § 340.
24. IEL §§ 346-351.
25. IEL §§ 352-359; Jacobs § 7.9.

In addition, there are anti-discrimination provisions in the NLRA, in Presidential Orders and in State laws.

American anti-discrimination law contains concepts that are very comparable with (but not identical to) those in Europe:

- direct vs indirect discrimination (*disparate impact*)[26];
- harassment,
- justifications for unequal treatment (e.g. the *bonafide occupational qualification*)[27],
- shifting the burden of proof to the employer[28],
- affirmative action (*reverse discrimination*)[29],
- victimisation (*retaliation*).[30]

Most cases of unequal treatment are finally solved by monetary compensation. In 2009, after the highly publicised Lilly Ledbetter case Congress adopted and President Obama signed the Fair Pay Act, amending all four Anti-discrimination Acts to make the statute of limitations more claimant-friendly in discrimination cases.[31]

Very important for the enforcement of these Acts all over the United States is the Federal Equal Employment Opportunity Commission (EEOC) (see par. 1.3). Moreover, there are state Equal Employment Opportunity Commissions[32]. Private enforcement suits are available in state or in federal courts, but also the EEOC itself can bring enforcement actions.

Remarkable differences with European anti-discrimination law are:

- There is still no general express prohibition of discrimination based on sexual orientation in Federal law, but they sometimes appear in Presidential Orders or State law;[33]
- The ADEA only prohibits age discrimination over 40 years; in Europe this is irrespective a certain age limit;[34]

26. IEL §§ 321-323/331-332; Jacobs § 7.2. ; In Lewis v. City of Chicago, 560 U.S. 205 (2010), the Supreme Court allowed a disparate impact claim on behalf of job applicants.

27. IEL §§ 324-326.

28. Jacobs § 7.3.

29. IEL §§ 327-330; Jacobs § 7.12.

30. IEL § 345.

31. IEL § 364.

32. IEL §§ 951-970.

33. IEL § 340; Jacobs § 7.10.

34. Jacobs § 7.8.

- Different from several countries in Europe the ADA offers no preferential treatment in the hiring of workers and the Act contains no quota.
- In the USA there are more discrimination claims than in Europe, because other grounds for claims (for instance in dismissal cases, see 2.21) are less developed that in Europe. Also damages for discrimination can often be higher than in other cases and in Europe.

Over the last fifty years the entire US Discrimination Law has developed into a huge building of legal wisdom. And there is still a lot of debate about technicalities. For instance, the case law about the standards of proof if an act (such as a dismissal) had a mixed motivation. U.S courts then usually apply the "but-for causation" standard, meaning that a plaintiff must show that age/sex/disability was *the* reason for the incriminated act, not that age/sex/disability was one of multiple reasons.

Another issue is whether the general prohibition of "disparate impact" also applies to job-applicants who are not yet employees.

So, many Americans are still not satisfied and fighting for more equality. Usually, the Democrats are supporting a further expansion of the equality rights while Republicans are reluctant. So, for instance affirmative action, a theme that for many years has been popular among Democrats[35], has in recent years lost support.

In these years with its numerous blockades at the Federal political level (see 1.1.2.) no substantial further expansion of the Federal law is possible. Therefore, Democrats are using their influence to expand equality law on the level of the States, which they control politically, and sometimes by Presidential Orders and in the various Federal agencies.

For instance, when the Democrats were in power (2009-2017) they have tried by administrative decisions and by nominations by the Obama Administration to stamp out LGBTQ-discriminations by giving an extensive interpretation of the prohibition of "sex" discrimination in the Civil Rights Act (Executive Order 13672 of 2014).

Under the Trump Administration several of these Federal protections of LGBTQ Americans have been dismantled. This Administration has repeatedly taken the position that laws and regulations that prohibit discrimination of the basis of sex do not protect a person discriminated for being gay or transgender.

35. T.M. Dworkin and others, Career Mentoring for Women: New Horizons/Expanded Methods.

However, finally in *Bostock v. Clayton Cty.*, 140 S. Ct. 1731 (2020), the U.S. Supreme Court ruled, 7-2, that the federal statute prohibiting discrimination based on sex is violated when an employee is dismissed for being homosexual or transgender. It explained that "sex plays a necessary and undisguisable role in the [employer's] decision" and, therefore, violates the statutory prohibition against discrimination based on sex. Thus, the federal laws as currently interpreted prohibit discrimination based on sexual orientation.

Pursuant this case, President Biden, shortly after his inauguration, issued Executive Order 13988, requiring all federal agencies to extend existing protections on the basis of sex to include sexual orientation and gender identity. Biden also wants Congress to pass the Equality Act, which would amend existing civil rights law to explicitly include sexual orientation and gender identification as protected characteristics. This bill is already passed the House but still faced with the filibuster obstacle in the Senate.

2.6. Wages – definition and protection

Like in Europe, in the USA too, the precise definition of wage is far from uniform, not only at Federal level but also in the various States. It varies with the legislative instrument in which it is used.[36]

In the USA the most comprehensive protection of the wage can be found in the wage payment statutes of the various States.[37] Connecticut for instance has laws which oblige the employer to pay its employees weekly all wages due to a regular pay day designated by the employer. When an employer discharges an employee, the employer must pay the employee all wages due no later than the end of the next business day. Moreover, Connecticut law prohibits an employer to deduct a number of items from the wages of an employee unless the employee has signed a form approved by the Connecticut Department of Labour. Employers are obliged to provide employees with each wage payment a statement of wages (itemized pay stub), etc.

At Federal level there is also a protection against deductions in the FLSA and a limitation on wage garnishment in the Federal Consumer Credit Protection Act.[38]

36. IEL § 284.

37. IEL § 288; Jacobs § 9.9.

38. Jacobs § 9.9.

In addition, there is a certain priority for wage claims under the Federal Bankruptcy Code, but this priority may often be illusory.[39] There exists, different from the EU Directive 2008/94/EC and from the principles in ILO-Convention 173, no USA-wide regulation of wage guarantee funds in bankruptcy cases.[40]

An important rule of ancient labour law in Europe and the USA has been: No work no pay. In the course of time everywhere labour law has made a lot of incursions on that rule, providing for sick pay, holidays with pay, etc. In the United States there are very few federal laws on that issue. Most precise rules on the continuation of wage payments are included in collective agreements[41] or in State law.

A typical American variation of such incursions on the no-work-no-pay-rule was the effort of trade unions to establish minimum standards specifying the number of certain employees who would have to be engaged and paid, work or no work. It was popularly called: "featherbedding" (sleeping on a feather bed and being paid for work). After a highly publicized court case the 1948 NLRA/LMRA made it an unfair labour practice for a trade union to cause an employer to pay for services which are not performed (s 8(b)(6). Fortunately, the courts have read it a narrowly.[42]

2.7. Minimum wage

The USA has a statutory minimum wage since 1938 contained in the Fair Labour Standards Act (FLSA).[43] Actually it still stands at $7.25 an hour, at which it was brought under President Obama in 2009! The FLSA provides that changes in the minimum wage are made by the Congress. The procedure is more politicised in the USA than in Europe.[44] The Obama administration further managed to bring the minimum wage for federal employees and contractors at $10.10 by an Executive Order of 2014. The Trump Administration did not take action on this point and now the Biden Administration is confronted with the old problem. It only could elevate the minimum Wage to $15 for Federal employees and contractors

39. IEL § 300-301; P.M. Secunda, An Analysis of the Treatment of Employee Pension and Wage Claims in Insolvency and Under Guarantee Schemes in OECD Countries: Comparative Law Lessons for Detroit and the United States, 41 Fordham Urb. L.J. 867 (2014).

40. Jacobs § 9.10.

41. IEL §§ 655-661.

42. IEL § 731; Jacobs § 9.11.

43. IEL §§ 84-91; Jacobs § 9.7.

44. IEL § 84.

by way of Executive Orders of 2022, but attempts for a general elevation of the Federal Minimum Wage to $15 by way of the "Raise the Wage Act" is stalled in Congress because the opposition of the Republicans is blocking it by the filibuster. Republican lawmakers continue to argue that $15 is an arbitrary political number that would have unintended economic consequences, including burdening small business by increasing costs and reducing employment.

In 2017 the FLSA minimum wage was about 28% of the mean hourly wage for such workers. At $7.25 an hour, a worker who is employed 40 hours a week for 52 weeks will annually earn $15,080. This is above the 2017 official poverty level for a single person household ($12,060) but below the level for a household of two persons ($16,240) and far below the level for a household of two adults with two children under 18 ($24,600).[45] A 40-hours work week with a minimum wage of $15 an hour comes out to an annual salary of about $31.000. That salary would be just above the federal poverty lines for a family of four, which is $27.750 a year.

27 States have established a State Minimum Wage at a higher level than the Federal minimum wage of $7.25, e.g. Washington $14,49, California $14, Massachusetts $14.25, Colorado $12.56, Maine $ 12.75; several states have the same as the federal minimum, like, Texas $7,25.[46] The procedures of adaptation of the State minimum wages varies considerably.

Several cities have fixed an even higher *living wage*, which is only binding for enterprises that do business with the municipality.[47]

As the FLSA is also applicable on the civil servants of the Federation and the States[48] it covers (2017) 130 million workers, over 85% of the labour force. Although the FLSA has one of the broadest definitions of "employees", there are several exceptions in this Act. First the companies not engaged in interstate commerce (see 1.2.1.) and further agriculture, fishing, educational enterprises, etc). Moreover, the Department of Labour allows employers to lawfully pay a reduced minimum wage to learners, apprentices, messengers, full-time students, the handicapped, etc.

The FLSA also limits the types of deductions that may be taken which reduce wages below the minimum, and requires that for employment

45. IEL § 40.

46. You can find the latest data at: https://www.minimum-wage.org/wage-by-state.

47. IEL § 178.

48. IEL § 91.

beyond 40 hours per week an added premium be paid equal to one-half of the regular wage rate (see 2.9).

The Administrator of the Wage and Hour Division of the Department of Labour is responsible for discovering, investigating and remedying violations of the FLSA. Employees may bring their own private suit in federal or state court.[49]

2.8. Equal Pay for equal work m/f

Equal pay for equal work m/f is regulated by the Equal Pay Act (EPA)1963.[50] Although the Act is in fact an amendment act on the FLSA, contrary to the other provisions of the FLSA it covers all workers.

Various definitions in the Equal Pay Act differ from those in the EU, notably on the fact that the federal USA concept of equality is related to equal work and not also to work of the same value ("that is substantially equal") as in the EU.[51]

Some States have Equal pay m/f legislation which is more progressive.

The EEOC is responsible for discovering, investigating and remedying violations of the FLSA equal pay provisions. Employees may bring their own private suit in federal or state court.[52]

In the USA, like in Europe, the gender wage gap has substantially been reduced since the Equal Pay Act was enacted in 1963: A reduction from ca. 60% to actually 82%. Today, on average, a woman working full time earns 82 cents for every dollar a man working full time earns.

That gap can be larger or smaller, depending on the state someone lives in. In Louisiana, for instance, the gender pay gap is 31.2%, the biggest wage gap in the nation. California has the smallest pay gap at 10.9%. US cities show an even greater range of pay discrepancy. Asian women face the smallest wage gap – they earn 97% of what white men earn, resulting in a pay gap of just 3%. White women earn 79%, while black women earn 67% and Hispanic women earn 58% of what white men do.[53]

For long years there was never any broad action by the federal governments to narrow the gap between principle and reality. Finally, it was the Obama Administration that made an Order to require from

49. IEL §§ 913-914; Jacobs § 9.7.

50. IEL §§ 84-91/360-364; Jacobs § 9.8.

51. IEL § 362.

52. IEL §§ 913-914; Jacobs § 9.7.

53. Business Insider, 26 August 2019.

companies doing business with the Federal government with at least 100 workers to publish their gender and racial wage figures. However, the Trump Administration decided in August 2017 to revoke this Order, but the Biden Administration has restored this Executive Order.

There are still several legal problems with the Equal Pay Act. One actual legal issue is, whether a pay discrepancy can be justified because it is based on "a person's *prior* salary history". While the EPA mandates equal pay for equal work, it provides employers some flexibility in setting wages. Employers can justify wage differentials if those differentials are based on things like seniority, merit, or "any other factor other than sex."

In the Rizo case[54], the employer argued that taking into account a persons' prior salary history and applying that factor consistently among employees regardless of sex, was not a "sex-based" wage determination in violation of the EPA.

Meanwhile, several cities and states have banned or are considering banning salary history inquiries by employers, including California[55], Massachusetts, Oregon, New Orleans, Philadelphia, and New York City.[56] President Biden signed an Executive Order that encourages the government to consider banning federal contractors from seeking information about job applicants' prior salary history in hiring and the pay-setting processes for workers.

In the US Congress there is still the Paycheck Fairness Act, already adopted in the House, but waiting for a filibuster-proof majority in the Senate. This Bill would provide more efficient remedies to victims of discrimination in the payment of wages on the basis of sex. This Bill aims to restrict the use of the "factor other than sex" defence to wage discrimination claims to "bona fide, job-related factors". Moreover, it would enhance non-retaliation prohibitions and make it unlawful to require an employee to sign a contract or waiver prohibiting the employee from disclosing information about the employee's wages. Finally, it would increase civil penalties for violations of equal pay provisions.

---

54. US Supreme Court, 25 February 2020; this Court remanded the case for further proceedings to the Appeals Court concerned because of a technical flaw.
55. Ca. Labor Code Section 432.3, AB 168 of 2018; Fair Pay Act Bill,2019; D. Hansen and D. McNichols, Information and the Persistance of the Gender Wage Gap: early Evidence from California's Salary History Ban, National Bureau of Economic Research, Cambridge, 2020.
56. S. Sinha, Salary History Ban: Gender Pay Gap and Spillover Effects, Yale University, 2019.

2.9. Working Time

In the USA there is no comprehensive Working Time legislation at Federal level. There are only Federal Working Time rules for certain sectors such as transport and certain groups such as youngsters (in the FLSA).[57]

Most States have a State Law on Working Times and also the collective agreements[58] usually contain rules on working times.

Very important, however is the rule in the Federal FLSA which requires a 50% extra wage for overtime work (over 40 hours a week) of lower paid workers. Under the Obama Administration the Democrats extended its application by increasing the maximum statutory threshold (from $23.660 to $ 47,476) but this was turned back by a federal judge. The Trump Administration then raised the threshold from $23.660 to $35.568 but this is not to the satisfaction of the Biden Administration.[59] This administration is expected to further raise the threshold later this year.

For already many years employers and Republicans would like to soften this provision by a so-called Working Families Flexibility Bill which would let employees who work overtime choose paid time off rather than time-and-a-half wages. Such a possibility exists already for civil servants and Republicans would like to extend this to the private sector. Trade unions and Democrats mistrusted this change and were able to stop this bill after it had already passed the House in 2017.

All in all, in the USA the regulation of working hours is much weaker than in Europe, which may be a cause for the fact that on average an employee in the USA is working more hours a year than his European colleague: ca. 2000 hours a year versus 1500-1800 hours a year in Europe. Consequently, American workers have on average more purchasing power, but are they also as healthy as their European colleagues?

2.10. Paid vacation

There are in the US no Federal rules on paid vacation (as in the EU Directive on Working Time).[60] Some States have statutes on paid vacation and most collective agreements[61] and company handbooks give workers the right to ca. 2 or 3 weeks of vacation with pay each year. As a result, 75%

57. Jacobs § 10.1.
58. IEL §§ 662-667.
59. IEL § 85.
60. Jacobs § 10.2.
61. IEL §§ 668-680.

of the America workers are entitled to 10 days of vacation after one year of service; 15 days after 5 year of service; 20 days after 20 years of service.[62] However, 25% of the American workers have no paid vacation right at all.

2.11. Leave regulations

At Federal level there are not many leave regulations. The US and Papua New Guinea seem to be the only countries in the world that even don't have paid maternity leave programs written into the highest law of the land.[63] The main Federal Act in this field is the Family and Medical Leave Act 1993 (FMLA), which provides for at least 12 weeks of *unpaid* leave for medical and family reasons. And even 44% of US workers don't have access to FLMA, because they work part-time, haven't been with their employer for at least a year, or work for smaller companies that are excluded from the program. More generous leave regulations are often included in States statutes or in collective agreements.

Democrats, some Republicans and even Ivanka Trump have more federal rules on leave promoted, but it could only be realised for Federal employees: The Federal Employee Paid Leave Act, 5 U.S.Code § 6382(a)(1), adopted in 2020, grants up to 12 weeks of paid parental leave to most federal government employees in connection with a child's birth or placement for adoption or foster care. Nine states with large populations (for example, California, New York, New Jersey, and Washington) also have programs for private sector employees to receive at least partial pay for parental leaves. Only 23% of private-sector workers have access to paid family leave; 60% do not have medical leave; 22% have no paid sick leave.

Biden's proposed Build Back Better Act sought to provide national paid family leave of 12 weeks. However, this massive $2 trillion social spending bill is struggling in Congress, failing to gain support not only from Republicans, but also from Democratic Senator Joe Manchin. There are some chances that this Bill can be passed in the weeks to come in a very compromise setting: perhaps only 4 weeks paid family leave.

2.12. Health and safety at work

In the past, like all European nations also the USA have been plagued by the high toll of occupational accidents. Now the number of fatal industrial accidents is down from 18 workers a year per 100,000 workers in 1970 to 3,5 workers in 2019.

62. IEL § 295-296.

63. Jacobs § 10.2.

To some extent this result may be attributed to State and federal workers' compensations laws and to the Occupational Safety and Health Act (OSHA) of 1970.[64] State workers' compensation laws provide very modest monetary recoveries for work related injuries and generally allow suits against the injured worker's employer or co-workers only in the event of gross negligence or intentional injury.

This federal OSHA imposes on the employer a huge responsibility for the worker's health, safety and property. The standards are not only in the Act. Especially in this field secondary legislation must provide for more precise rules. Such rules are – at federal level – drawn up by the Secretary of Labour and the Occupational Safety and Health Review Commission.

Apart from several other limitations[65] the federal OSHA has the usual limitation that it is only applicable to employers involved in interstate commerce. Therefore, most States have issued comparable rules to cover other business and some States have issued rules that are more far-reaching. But not only that. In order to respect the different needs of various States the federal OSHA has permitted the State to adopt its own program to regulate workers' health and safety instead of the federal rules, if the State program is approved by the federal Secretary of Labour as being at least as effective as the federal program. For instance, California did so in view of its experience with great seismic instability. Actually ca. 21 States operate such own State OSHA programs. Nationwide operating companies not always see this respect for State autonomy as an advantage.[66]

The federal Secretary of Labour and the Occupational Safety and Health Review Commission are also responsible for the enforcement of the federal rules in this area (comparable with the Labour Inspectorate in EU countries). The OSHA rules are enforced through abatement orders requiring the removal or reduction of hazardous conditions and through the assessment of civil and criminal penalties.[67] However there is a lot of criticism on the quality of enforcement of OSHA rules. An American employer on average can assume that it has less than 2% chance of being inspected during a year. Moreover, State programs do not provide for enforcement as rigorous as the federal program. For civil law suits it can be useful, that often the company handbook gives express or implied assurance that the employer will protect the workers' welfare.

64. IEL § 274-276.

65. IEL § 227-230/945-950; Jacobs §§ 10.3/10.4.

66. IEL § 947..

67. IEL §§ 921-950/274.

2.13. Liability for mistakes by the workers

Like in Europe also in the USA the main rule is: the employer is most of the times liable for damages resulting from mistakes made by his employees in the course of their employment (*respondeat superior*). Besides that, also the worker is liable for his own misconduct even though he is acting while in the course of his employment and at the specific directions of his employer.

There are no Federal rules in this field. The limitations and the exceptions of this principle vary somewhat from one State to the other because this is all judge-made common law![68]

2.14. The management right of the employer

In the USA this right is a source of rules in employment relationships perhaps even more forceful than in Europe. Even collective agreements often open with a broad clause recognising the management right of the employer. Nevertheless, unions frequently try to limit certain aspects of managerial authority to make core business decisions.[69]

The right to take disciplinary actions against an employee is one of the aspects of the wide managerial right of the employer. Warnings, demotions, suspensions from work, denial of wage increases, and cancellations of privileges are examples of the many methods by which employers are able to maintain work force discipline.[70] Dismissal is the most extreme form of disciplinary power. Often the company handbooks describe the employer's policies.

However, there are limits upon the disciplinary discretion of the employer in civil law, in the anti-victimisation measures contained in statutes, in the wage legislation, and in the collective agreements.[71]

And often collective agreements or company handbooks are cushioning this right with procedural rules.

2.15. Modification of the contract of employment

Obviously, the employer cannot change the working conditions below the standards set by federal and State labour law. And in companies under a collective agreement no terms of conditions of employment may be

68. IEL § 277-282; Jacobs § 10.9.

69. IEL § 725; Jacobs § 10.8.

70. IEL § 145/696.

71. IEL § 145/694.

modified contrary to the collective agreement or without the agreement of the union (see further 3.3.3).[72]

Besides these restrictions – which for many American workers are not very helpful – American employers have a large space to modify unilaterally the content of the contracts of employment of their workers. Thanks to the broad right of management in the USA, broader than that in Europe.

There are no Federal rules and few State rules restraining this freedom in more general terms; it is all common law that may slightly vary from one State to another. There may be a growing number of state courts that restrict the employers' authority to unilaterally modify employment contracts.[73] However, most courts still take the position that allows unilateral modifications by the employer but only where it is not motivated by bad faith and the employee has given sufficient notice before the change becomes effective.[74]

2.16. Transfer of enterprises

Very much different from the situation in Europe [where there is the EU Directive on transfer of enterprises] in the USA there is no Federal law imposing on the transferee the obligation to take over all the personnel of the transferor and to maintain provisionally their existing terms of employment.

The US Supreme Court has once pronounced that such a rule does not exist in the federal law of the USA[75], but it is sometimes in collective agreements.[76]

Somewhat less freedom is left to an employer that effectively has taken over (most of) the employees of the transferor. Not always, but sometimes he may be bound to the collective agreement concluded by the transferor.

2.17. Non-compete agreements

In the USA *non-compete agreements or Covenants Non to Compete* are not unusual. They are not governed by Federal law but by State law (sometimes State Acts, sometimes judge-made) which differs a little bit from State to State.

72. IEL § 366.

73. IEL § 129;

74. IEL § 148; Jacobs § 10.11.

75. Jacobs § 8.12.

76. IEL §§ 639-644.

In general, such agreements are regarded by the courts with great suspicion as they are contrary to very American notions like *no restraints of trade* and *the freedom to hire and fire*. However, they are enforced by the courts if the restriction is no greater than is necessary for the protection of some legitimate interest of the former employer, does not impose undue hardship on the worker and is not injurious to the public.[77]

At one time non-compete agreements were mostly used for professional type positions like sales representatives, executives, doctors and lawyers. But in recent years, more employers have adopted the practice for a much wider range of employees, such as security guards, pre-school teachers, home health aides, sandwich shop workers, etc. It was estimated that now 16-18% of American workers have a non-compete agreement at their current jobs.

Several states have recently passed laws to curtail and limit the enforcement and application of non-compete clauses.

North Dakota and Oklahoma do not allow employers to use non-compete agreements. Oregon bans them for low-wage workers. In California, where non-compete clauses are not enforceable, ca. 45% of business use non-competition clauses. A new non-compete law in Illinois allows employees to recover their attorneys' fees and empowers the Attorney General's office to intervene to protect competition.

The Obama Administration sparked a national dialogue around these agreements.

On July 8, 2021, President Biden signed an Executive Order on Promoting Competition in the American Economy, in which the Federal Trade Commission is encouraged to curtail the unfair use of non-compete clauses and other clauses or agreements that may unfairly limit worker mobility.

In Congress there is now, with bipartisan support, the Workforce Mobility Bill, which seeks to rein in the use of non-compete agreements. Also, the Freedom to Compete Bill can potentially limit the use of non-compete agreements.

2.18. Patents and copy rights

An employee is entitled to keep his own discoveries (inventions) even tough made during the course of employment, unless the employment contract specifically provides otherwise or unless the employee is

77. IEL §§ 221-226; Jacobs § 10.7.

employed specifically for the purpose of applying his inventive capacity to produce an invention of the sort that is in dispute.[78]

For the intellectual creations the basic rule is the other way around. Under the federal Copyright Act, the employer is entitled to the copy right if the work was created within the scope of the employment, unless the employment contract specifically provides otherwise.[79]

2.19. Bona Fides

In many European states, courts assume that the contract of employment explicitly or implicitly is governed by the principle of *bona fides*. This means that an employer owes an employee a duty to act in good faith and to deal fairly with him/her. This principle goes both ways, meaning the employee has the same duty to the employer.

In the USA the legal requirement of good faith and fair dealing most often has been imposed through the law of torts. Moreover, the doctrine of good faith and fair dealing has been generally accepted in other types of contractual obligations, but only a few courts have found it applicable fully on the contract of employment. In several states, courts have refused to apply this principle to individual contracts of employment.[80]

Certainly, an implied covenant of good faith and fair dealing is not recognized as a cause of action in the courts of many American states. Only if such a covenant is laid down in a written employment contract then one may be able to file a claim against the other party if the other party didn't abide by the terms of the contract. Even then it takes serious wrongful conduct to violate the covenant of good faith and fair dealing.[81]

In result: in the USA judges may recognise that in principle *the duty of good faith and fair dealing* is applicable on the contract of employment, but even when they apply it they will do it only very marginally to the employer as they do not want to encroach too much upon the *management discretion* of the employer.[82]

78. IEL §§ 210-211; Jacobs § 10.10.

79. IEL §§ 212-214; Jacobs § 10.10.

80. Jacobs § 10.12.

81. D. Grossmann, Jettisoning the Normative Value of the Implied Duty of Good Faith, in Employee Rights and Employment Policy Journal, Vol. 21, No. 2, 2017; A. Bagchi, Unions and the Duty of Good Faith in Employment Contracts, Yale Law Journal, Vol. 112 [2003], p. 1881-1910.

82. IEL 149-153.

Judges are more ready to confront the employee with his/her *duty of loyalty*.[83] One of the aspects of this duty is the obligation on the worker to refrain from disclosure of trade secrets.[84] Workers who breach their duty of loyalty generally may be dismissed and forfeit their wages as well as the gains from the improper conduct.[85]

But now there are the federal and state Whistleblower Acts. At federal level there are the False Claim Reform Act of 1986, the Whistleblower Protection Act of 1989/2012 and the Sarbanes Oxley Act of 2002. These acts prohibit retaliation against the employee who reports wrongdoing on the part of an employer or high-ranking officials of the establishment. Whistleblower protecting is also provided for those seeking to vindicate their rights or assist in vindicating the rights of others under the most basic laws.[86]

Sometimes State law offers a broader protection to whistleblowers. In, for instance the State of New York, there is section 740 of the New York Labour Law, reformed on October 2021, which broadened the scope of Whistleblowers protection to any violation of federal laws, regulations of acts and also including former employees and independent contractors.

2.20. Privacy

The constitutional protection of privacy has been construed to extend to state and local government workers as a result of the protections afforded by the 14th Amendment. This rule can directly be invoked by civil servants of the federal government (see 1.3.). In private business there is some general federal privacy protection legislation.[87] For instance, there is the federal Electronic Communications Privacy Act (Wiretap Act) which may prohibit employers to secretly listening employee conversations. This Act is also applicable on employer monitoring of e-mail and voice mail of the employees.

American employers often resort to tests and investigations in an effort to determine whether a job applicant or an employee is an honest person. This is treated by some States as an interference with the worker's right of privacy. Most states have adopted a broad array of restrictions on employer

83. Frank J Cavico, a..o. The Duty of Loyalty in the Employment Relationship: Legal Analysis and Recommendations for Employers and Workers, Journal of Legal, Ethical and Regulatory Issues Volume 21, Issue 3, 2018, p. 2-27.

84. IEL §§ 215-222.

85. IEL § 206-208.

86. IEL §§ 158-162.

87. IEL §§ 244-250; Jacobs § 10.6.

use of such tests as well as regulations respecting the qualifications and the conduct of those who administer the tests. At federal level there is the Employee Polygraph Protection Act 1988, which imposes minimal restrictions on employer uses of polygraph ("lie detector") and related types of tests.

For the rest it is mainly State privacy law that governs the limitations on employee conduct both at and away from the workplace.[88] According to these laws generally employees have a right to a remedy (normally monetary damages) if the employers' intrusion on the employee's reasonable expectation of privacy is highly offensive and is not outweighed by any social interests that motivate the employers' conduct.

Employers often compile a broad range of information about an individual worker's prior experience, education, work performance, financial problems, legal problems, marital status, health history and the like. Concerns about employee privacy have recently intensified with the introduction of data analytic tools in the workplace. They may be addressed by the federal Fair Credit Reporting Act (FCRA) which also protects employee privacy by placing restrictions on employers' information gathering practices. Protection respecting the dissemination of employee medical information may come from ADA, the HIPAA and the Genetic Information Non-discrimination Act 2008.[89] Moreover the risks posed by data mining techniques can be addressed under the common law, which has several torts to offer. However, the application of these common law torts on privacy in the workplace is limited, as these torts are simply not geared toward this purpose. The United States has no omnibus data protecting regime like the EU (Re 2016/679/EU) has. There are federal laws regarding the protection of financial and medical data. Some States have their own data protection laws, which vary from State to State.

Finally, privacy questions are at stake concerning governmental and employers' interest to contain alcohol and drug abuses, because of the impact of these substances on public health and safety and employee health, safety and job performance. The federal government adopted in 1988 the Drug-Free Workplace Act, which requires all employers that contract with the federal government to ban the use, possession and distribution of illegal drugs from their premises. The federal Omnibus Transportation Employee Testing Act regulates when and how drug tests

88. IEL § 164.

89. IEL § 164; P.T. Kim, Data Mining and the Challenges of Protecting Employee Privacy Under U.S. Law, 40 Comp. Labour Law & Policy Journal 405 (2019), p. 405-419.

are administered to transportation workers. A number of States as well have statutes about drug testing.

2.21. The Law on Dismissals

2.21.1. The basic rule

In the European Union an employee in principle can only be dismissed if there is a good cause. In the USA the basis of the law on dismissals is still *the employment at will*, which means notably that every employer can dismiss a worker at any time for any reason.[90] This basic common law rule, adopted and elaborated by judges, was stated more than 130 years ago in the following terms: "Employment for an indefinite term is presumptively employment at will," and an employee can be dismissed "for good cause, no cause or even a cause morally wrong." This doctrine has been upheld in the name of furthering personal liberty and the right of property expressed through freedom of contract. For over 100 years, the courts nurtured this doctrine of employment at will, disclaiming any concern for justice or fairness and this doctrine continues to dominate the US law on dismissals to this day.

2.21.2. Deviations

However, in the last half century, many courts have carved out a number of deviations of this basic rule.

(a) Deviations in the individual contract of employment

It is possible that the individual contract of employment shows another arrangement. It may for instance mention a period of notice.[91]

(b) Deviations in the staff guide/company handbooks[92]

A company handbook typically contains the phrase that the employer expects that the employment relationship will be of long duration, but this was not seen as a deviation from the presumption of at-will-employment. Sometimes, however, company handbooks contain more explicit promises, such as the promise of the employer first to look for an alternative job before dismissing a worker or mentioning a period of notice.

90. IEL § 129; Jacobs § 12.1; C.W. Summers, Employment at will in the United States: The Divine Right of Employers, University of Pennsylvania Journal of Labour and Employment Law, 3(65), 2000.

91. Jacobs § 12.2.

92. Jacobs § 12.3.

Several courts have treated such representations in the handbooks as establishing enforceable contracts and ruled that employees can rely on it as a basis for legal redress if dismissed from employment in violation of such commitments (see 2.4). This has resulted in most handbooks now typically contain the disclaimer: "This handbook is only a statement of company policy and is not intended to create a contract." Most courts now hold that indeed the employer can escape the binding force of positive assurances made in the handbook by including such a disclaimer.[93]

(c) Deviations in the collective agreement

Most collective agreements nowadays contain deviations from the employment-at-will rule, e.g.

- by ordering a period of notice
- by providing for seniority rules in a collective dismissal
- by requiring a *justa causa* for a dismissal
- by referring to the good faith/fair dealing principle

However, remember that only 12% of American workers are covered by collective agreements.

(d) Deviations in statutory provisions[94]

There are many such deviations both in Federal law and in State law, e.g. in the FLSA, in Anti-Discrimination laws, such as the ADA which protects to a certain extent, sick and disabled workers against dismissal[95], the same effect has the FMLA. Also acts like the NLRA, the Whistleblower protection Acts, etc contain limits on the employers' freedom to fire.

Statutes often also contain anti-victimisation clauses which may prohibit a dismissal.

Several States have laws explicitly prohibiting employers from terminating employees in circumstances, like when the termination is based on the conduct of an employee outside the workplace.[96]

(e) Deviations by way of public policy or specific reasons[97]

93. IEL § 148; Jacobs § 12.4.

94. IEL § 156; Jacobs § 12.5.

95. IEL § 170.

96. IEL § 146, 156-158

97. IEL § 154-155; Jacobs § 12.6.

which may prohibit a dismissal of a worker who is dismissed because he refused to commit perjury or the screening by a lie detector or in a setting of defamation[98] or after an unfair examination of his case, etc.

One ought not assume too quickly that these reasons are applied. For almost every case in which one court has found a public policy violation, some other court faced with similar facts, has found no violation![99]

(f) Deviations because of the good cause principle.[100]

As we have seen above (under c. and in 2.19) the principle of "good faith and fair dealing" is very often laid down in the dismissal provisions of a collective agreement. Outside this area it is only in the State of Montana that first the judges and then the State legislature have adopted that this principle of "good faith and fair dealing" is implicit in every contractual relation and therefore that is should be applied in dismissal cases as well.[101] During the early 1980s when some courts adopted these exceptions, it was believed, or at least hoped, that the employment at will doctrine would be subordinated to considerations of justice. But it is clear now that most courts are not applying them at all or only scarcely. So, in result, this good cause deviation on employment at will provides little protection for the 90% of American workers that not are working under a collective agreement.

Finally: the party asserting that one of these 6 deviations are applicably has the burden to proof this.

2.21.3. Periods of notice

Individual contracts of employment, collective agreements or staff guides/ company handbooks may provide for an obligatory period of notice.[102] If such a period is not required, both the employer and the employee may immediately terminate the contract in individual dismissal cases.[103]

Federal law only provides a notice period in collective dismissals: the employer must at least 60 days before effectuating such a dismissal notify

98. IEL § 162-164.

99. IEL §§ 153-154.

100. IEL § 152; Jacobs § 12.7.

101. IEL § 145.

102. Jacobs § 12.9.

103. Jacobs § 12.10.

the trade unions and the local government (under the Federal Plant Closing Act, officially: Worker Adjustment and Retraining Notification Act [WARN). The act applies to enterprises with at least 100 full-time employees and to situations involving a plant closing affecting at least 50 full-time employees at an employment site (or comparable layoffs).[104]

Several State laws offer a better protection on this item.[105]

2.21.4. Other means to terminate a contract of employment

Besides these deviations of the termination at will doctrine there are obviously other variations on this theme possible.

Parties may terminate their contract by mutual agreement.[106]

Parties may have concluded a fixed term contract. The courts hold that either party may only rescind such a contract for good cause.[107]

Of course, the death of the employee and also of the employer automatically terminates the employment contract.[108]

Bankruptcy results in the termination on any employment contracts at the election of the court-appointed trustee.[109]

Parties may have agreed a probationary period.[110]

2.21.5. Remedies

A wrongly discharged worker employed under a contract for a specific duration is entitled to recover damages for the breach of contract. A worker whose employment contract was not for a specific duration, but whose termination violated other contractual commitments will usually recover lost earnings and related compensation losses.[111]

Reinstatement is a remedy that courts have normally not available in a tort or contract cause of action, but it is often available for breach of a statutory protection of worker interests (Title VII, ADA, ADEA, FLSA, FMLA, OSHA, NLRA). This remedy is also generally ordered by labour

104. IEL § 155; Jacobs § 12.11.

105. IEL § 155.

106. IEL § 174; Jacobs § 12.13.

107. IEL § 146; Jacobs § 12.14.

108. IEL § 172.

109. IEL § 173.

110. IEL § 654; Jacobs § 12.14.

111. IEL § 180-182; Jacobs § 12.15.

arbitrators where a worker has been discharged in breach of the collective agreement. Courts enforce such orders.[112]

2.22. Child Labour

The FLSA prohibits almost all employment of children under the age of 14, but provides for exceptions. For children at work between 14 and 18 years there are additional limitations on the general law limitations on work.[113]

State laws extend the coverage of these standards to all children in these age categories.

In the USA the legal capacity to contract begins at age 18, but there are exceptions for minors.[114]

2.23. Foreign workers

Although the USA traditionally has been a country open to mass immigration, since a hundred years it is very much limiting the access of foreigners to the American Labour market. The federal Immigration Reform and Control Act provides for various programs for authorizing limited groups of aliens the access to the American labour and prohibits employers the knowing employment of aliens unauthorized to work in the US. The employer must obtain from all workers (citizens and non-citizens alike) documentation which testify authorisation to work in the USA.

Nevertheless, there are presumably millions of unauthorized aliens working in the USA and there is much debate and uncertainty about the labour law rights of these persons.[115]

2.24. Job placement services

Already in the 19th century many initiatives were taken to bring offer and demand together on the American labour market. Notorious were the so-called hiring halls, many of them controlled by the unions.[116] A Federal employment service was created in 1933 by the Federal Employment Services Act. This Act has been many times reformed until in 2014

112. IEL §§ 183-186.

113. IEL § 90.

114. IEL § 130-132; Jacobs § 8.4.

115. IEL § 130; Jacobs § 8.5.

116. IEL § 650.

the Obama Administration had adopted by Congress the Workforce Innovation and Opportunity Act. Also, many States have organised their own service for the labour market, operating in conjunction with the administration of State unemployment compensation insurance.[117] So one of the aspirations of the new federal Workforce Innovation and Opportunity Act is to better integrate Federal and State programs for the labour market.

All these services must comply with the federal rules that prohibit each form of discrimination.[118]

In the US temporary work agencies is an ambiguous notion.[119] Some temporary workers are provided by companies that specialize in referring such workers but in other instances a company lends (assigns) its regular workers to another company for a period of time. Also, the data collection for these types of work arrangements often is unclear as to who provides the information and what definitions are used for workers secured through what are said to be temporary work agencies.

Jobs supplied by temporary agencies reached a record high of 3.2 million in 2018, but only three States, Massachusetts, Illinois and California have passed laws to rein in abuses in the temp and staffing industry and to provide some baseline protections for temp workers.

117. IEL § 742; Jacobs § 8.1.

118. IEL § 402.

119. Jacobs § 8.2.

CHAPTER III

(Collective) Labour Law

The USA has seen a stormy development of its industrial relations and collective labour law since the 19th century, which has culminated in a mayor Federal legal framework, the National Labour Relations Act.[1]

3.1. General

3.1.1. The NLRA/LMRA and the LMRDA

Collective labour law in the US is mainly based on one great Federal statute, the National Labour Relations Act (NLRA), incorporated in the Labour Management Relations Act (LMRA). It has its historic roots in the 1930s – the Great Depression Period. President Roosevelt launched this Act in order to support the trade unions. His philosophy was that the strength of trade unions was needed to stop the fall of employment and the purchasing power of the American people in these dark economic times.

Since 1934 there have been only 2 times important changes in the law, both because the 1934 Act was considered as too much tilted to the trade union side. In order to correct this there have been launched

- 1947 the Labour/Management Relations Act (LMRA) (Taft-Hartley Act)[2]

(which has in fact incorporated the NLRA[3]), notably to limit the right to strike;

- 1959 the Landrum-Griffin Act [the Labour-Management Reporting and Disclosure Act, LMRDA][4]

a sort of Bill of Rights for trade union members vis-à-vis the trade unions themselves because there has been a lot of talk on the abuse of trade union power.[5]

All these Acts have completely overruled all the common law and most State laws in the field of collective labour relations in the US. State law only plays a marginal role. From New York to California there is a 95% uniform system at least for the middle-sized and large companies (for the exceptions see par. 3.1.5).

1. Jacobs § 2.1.
2. C. Gordon, The Legacy of Taft-Hartley, https://jacobinmag.com/2017/12/taft-hartley-unions-right-to-work.
3. The NLRA is now a 'title' or portion of the LMRA, see IEL §§ 81/749.
4. IEL § 444-/504-533.
5. IEL § 517.

Many observers believe that the NLRA is very much outdated and no longer fulfilling the aspirations of the American society. In the course of time many proposals have been made to amend this legislation. Since 1959 all this in vain as far as fundamental issues were concerned.[6] A more fundamental reform is apparently impossible in view of the political situation (see 1.1.2). The US Congress recently debated an Employee Rights Bill (that had the support of the Trump Administration) to bring about several changes in the NLRA, but with the House majority since 2018 in Democrat hands this Bill could not pass. Now under the Biden Administration the Democrats have presented their views on a drastic reform of the NLRA in the so-called Protecting the Right to Organize Bill (PRO-Act). This bill has already passed the House but is now confronted with stiff opposition of the Republicans who are determined to filibuster it.

3.1.2. The hard core: Art. 7 NLRA

The fundamental basis of the American system of collective labour relations is in the first part of Article 7 NLRA. It literally reads:

> *"Employees shall have the right*
> *- to self-organization, to form, join or assist labour organizations,*
> *- to bargain collectively through representatives of their own choosing, and*
> *- to engage in concerted activities for the purpose of collective bargaining or other mutual aid or protection...".*

These words embrace the right to (trade union) association, the right to collective bargaining and the right to strike.

In Europe, these rights are often enshrined in the Constitutions of the nations and in Charters of the European Organisations. In the US they are only laid down in a simple Act of Parliament, the NLRA/LMRA.

In addition, the NLRA created a somewhat bureaucratic system to let those rights flourish, not in wilderness but in orderly practice, geared towards producing collective agreements. This notably by imposing on the employers a duty to bargain (see 3.3.3) with the union that has the support of the majority of the workers (see 3.3.5).

3.1.3. Enforcement

As the NLRA overruled completely the common law it needed an own system of enforcement. Encroachments of the rights and obligations

6. Jacobs § 2.9.

of the NLRA are called "*unfair labour practices*" and enforced by orders to abstain from those practices and to pay *fines*.[7]

And the system of duties to bargain with the union that has the support of the majority of the workers clearly required a powerful institution to make it work in practice.

For both functions the NLRA established a special agency, the nation-wide operating National Labour Relations Board (NLRB)[8], that is charged with the application, interpretation and enforcement of the NLRA.

One of the most important activities of this Board are in the organisation of elections in enterprises to select the union which is supported by the majority of the workers (see 3.3.5).

With respect to violations of unfair labour practices, either by the employer or by the union, the NLRB provides a remedy through an unfair labour practice proceeding.

This procedure may be started by charges that can made by every concerned citizen or group to the NLRB or by the Board on its own initiative. If after a first inquiry the charge seem well founded the NLRB will issue an official complaint. That will be heard by an Administrative Law Judge who will first seek conciliation. If that is not possible, he will give his verdict, which – if the charge is confirmed - will normally be a cease and desist order and an order to undo any damage. If necessary, this verdict can be enforced by court decree. The concerned parties may also appeal to this verdict to the NLR Board. The decisions of the NLRB are reviewable in the Federal Courts of Appeal and the US Supreme Court.

All this, however, does not private a cause of action by an employee against the employer or the union.[9] The NLRA prohibits an employer from imposing any sanction on an employee because that individual has filed charges based on the NLRA with the NLRB or the courts.[10]

So, in theory the NLRB is a very powerful institute and therefore one can understand that subsequent Presidential administrations have always tried to influence the direction of the NLRB decisions by their power to nominate the members and especially the chairman of this institution (see 1.1.2). And there have been several occasions in which either the

7. IEL §§ 77.
8. IEL §§ 798-812; Jacobs § 2.2/11.5.
9. IEL §§ 548-549/777/794/803-811.
10. IEL §§ 491-492.

Republicans/employers or the Democrats/trade unions have tried to block the appointment of members/chairman of the NLR Board.

3.1.4. Exceptions in the scope of the NLRA

One of the exceptions is the result of the 'interstate commerce' exception (see 1.2.1). Companies that are not engaged in interstate commerce are outside the scope of the NLRA. The NLRB uses here guideline criteria based on the type of industry and the level of business activity. For instance: orchestra musicians are only covered if the annual receipts of the orchestra exceed $ 1 million, employees of hotels if the hotel has gross annual turnover of more than $ 500.000.[11]

Expressly excluded from the scope of the NLRA are household servants, farm workers, and supervisors.[12]

In the air and rail transportation industries, although the substantive protections of collective activity by workers are largely the same, the procedures for establishing union representation and engaging in collective bargaining are different from that of employment in the rest of private sector employment.[13]

In public sector collective employee representation - although there are some similarities with the private sector, such as the rule that only a union with majority support has the right to engage in collective bargaining - not all states recognize the right to collective employee representation and the procedures for establishing a union's majority status and engaging in collective bargaining are different from that of employment in the private sector and vary from state to state.[14]

Independent workers are not covered by the NLRA. However, in nowadays labour markets there are a lot of "contractors", which are often called independents but in the eyes of the trade unions they are effectively employees.

This has created the problem of "misclassification", which we have described in par. 2.2. For this reason the Democrats on Capitol Hill are trying in the PRO-Act to redefined the term "contractor" under the NLRA on the model of California Act AB and limit "contract work" to "(A) jobs free from control or direction of the hiring entity in connection of the performance of the work" (B) "jobs performed outside the normal

11. IEL § 781; Jacobs § 2.3.
12. IEL § 377; 417-421/608-609; Jacobs § 2.3.
13. IEL §§ 515-517/780; Jacobs § 2.3/2.5/2.6/2.7.
14. IEL §§ 596-605/621-628 for collective bargaining for public employees.

scope of the hiring entity's business" and (C) jobs "in which the worker is routinely doing work in an independently established trade, occupation or profession of the same nature of the work performed."

3.1.5. State Law

The pre-emptive impact of federal labour law (see 1.3.) has substantially limited the extent to which labour organisations and management-labour relations are subject to the body of state law in this field.[15] However, there is a major role left for State law in all the sectors where the NLRA-LMRA and the LMRDA do not apply.[16]

3.2. Trade Unions and Trade Unions Rights

As we have seen the first aim of the NLRA is to protect the right of the workers to self-organization, to form, join or assist labour organizations.

3.2.1. Trade Unions

American trade unions have a rich history.[17] Nowadays there are ten thousand of trade unions in the US, mostly local unions[18] and further organised in mainly national sector or professional trade unions, like the International Brotherhood of Teamsters or the American Federation of Teachers.

Most of them are loosely united in the main Trade Union Confederation AFL-CIO, which are comprising unions with, in total, circa 13 million members. The AFL-CIO has a vibrant history of secessions and mergers.[19] In 2005 there was the most recent secession, when 7 unions under leading of the International Brotherhood of Teamsters ran away and established the Change-to-Win Federation.[20] After in later years some trade unions withdrew from the Change-to-Win Federation, it now still counts unions with some 5 million members.

15. IEL §§ 825-827.
16. Jacobs § 2.4.
17. IEL § 497; Jacobs § 3.1; See G.W. Domhoff, The Rise and Fall of Labour Unions in the U.S. from the 1830s until 2012, in Who Rules America, https://whorulesamerica.ucsc.edu/power/history_of_labor_unions.html
18. IEL § 497/504/514.
19. IEL §§ 498-514; Jacobs § 3.2.
20. IEL §§ 64-67.

3.2.2. Rate of organisation

The rate of organisation among workers is low: ca. 10%[21], and it varies across the U.S. It is strongest in the North-Eastern and most Western States and is weak in most Mid-West and Southern States. It is quite high in the public service (34%) and therefore it is probably in the private sector about 6%.

3.2.3. Employers' associations

Many employers have joint forces in employers' associations that exist in almost every industry. At national level they are represented by the Chamber of Commerce and the National Association of Manufacturers.[22]

3.2.4. Legal rules on trade unions

Basically, trade unions are regulated in accordance with the common law on private organisations. It allows them a great liberty in their own intern charters and by-laws. They can sue and be sued in court. Most internal rights of the members of trade unions are standardised by the LMRDA.[23]

Because, as we will see in next Chapter (3.3.5), only the majority trade union can conclude collective agreements, the majority union has a duty of fair representation. It has to fairly represent all workers covered by the collective agreement, regardless of their membership or non-membership in this union.[24]

All trade union rights vis-à-vis the employers are laid down in the NLRA, in decisions of the NLRB and in the federal court cases. There is a long case law on these provisions.[25]

3.2.5. No interference with workers trade union rights and no discrimination

The NLRA prohibits employers from interfering with, restraining or coercing with the trade union rights of unions and employees. It further prohibits employers from encouraging or discouraging union membership by discriminating with respect to hiring, job tenure or conditions of employment (Art. 8 NLRA).[26]

21. IEL §§ 42/494-497.

22. IEL §§ 554-559.

23. IEL §§ 518-539.

24. IEL §§ 540-541/551-553.

25. IEL §§ 432-443.

26. IEL §§ 393-397; Jacobs § 3.4.

Nevertheless, there is still a long story of employers trying to deter their workers to get unionised and to avoid the engagement of unionised workers. Employers invoke their Constitutional freedom of expression to do such kind of things.[27] And they try to get rid of employees that are unionised, to prevent unions to enter the enterprise etc. American employers are badly reputed for these practices of "union bashing". Many law firms are specialised in advising the employers the best tactics to do so within the margins of the law.[28]

You can get a good picture of these practices in the documentary "American Factory".[29]

The basic remedy for unfair labour practices of the employer which has dismissed or disadvantaged a worker is: reinstatement with all the rights and privileges to which the employee would be entitled.[30] However, a victimized union member has a much more difficult burden of proof than victims of discrimination. An employer can be found in violation of the NLRB only if it is proven by a preponderance of evidence that the employer intended to discriminate for union activity.[31]

The PRO-Act aims to authorize meaningful penalties for employers that violates workers' rights. And it requires the NLRB to immediately seek an injunction to reinstate workers who suffer retaliation for exercising their rights. It allows workers to seek justice in court when employers unlawfully interfere with their NLRA rights or retaliate against them for enforcing NLRA rights. The Bill prevents workers being denied remedies due to their immigration status. It requires employers to post notices that inform workers of their rights under the NLRA and to disclose contracts with consultants hired to persuade employees on how to exercise their rights.

3.2.6. Facilities for trade unions

Trade unions would generally insist on access to worker names and addresses, and to employees on the employer's premises and via internal communication services, like company bulletin boards and intranet. Most employers object this, invoking the Constitutional rights on privacy, right of property, etc. Federal law does not contain special provisions

27. IEL §§ 377-392.

28. IEL §§ 374, A.J. Boling and others, Labour and Employment Compliance in the United States,- Kluwer Law International, The Hague, 2020.

29. Reichert J. & Bognar, S. (Directors), 2019, American Factory, Higher Ground Productions on Netflix.

30. IEL §§ 407-409/803-804.

31. IEL §§ 378-379.

on that, the case law is poor and not all collective agreements are much more generous on this item.[32]

3.2.7. Protection against unions

However, also trade unions are not always right. Therefore, also unions are prohibited from restraining or coercing workers in the exercise of their rights. So, e.g. union coercion to gain employee support or to deter them from supporting a rival union is an unfair labour practice.[33]

In the past many American unions were undemocratic and corruptive. The already mentioned 1959 Federal Statute (the Labour Management Reporting and Disclosure Act; the Landrum-Griffin Act, LMRDA) requires that the internal processes of unions should be democratic.[34]

The LMRDA is administered and enforced by the Department of Labour; the NLRB plays no role in it. The Department will act upon its own investigations and complaints of concerned citizens or groups. Private union members can also enforce their rights vis-à-vis the trade unions by filing a suit in federal District Courts. If violations are established the concerned unions are ordered to pay compensation and punitive damages. A number of the LMRDA provisions impose criminal penalties on wilful violations. They are prosecuted by the US District Attorneys.[35]

3.2.8. The closed shop etc.

The American labour movement has a long tradition of protecting their own strength by convening closed shop rules in collective agreements. The NLRA was condoning this practice (in the last words of the text Art. 7 NLRA) but the LMRA and the case law has established that a union may not request or require an employer to discharge an employee for non-membership. However, the courts have accepted a kind of closed shop-light: called agency shop. A collective bargaining provision that on its face requires a worker to become and remain a union member with the only obligation that the non-unionised employees must pay their share of the costs of the union.[36]

In 27 Republican-dominated States so-called Right-to-Work Laws have been adopted that even outlaw such agency shops. This has provoked

32. IEL §§ 432-444/726; Jacobs § 3.4.

33. IEL § 378; Jacobs § 3.3.

34. Jacobs § 3.5.

35. IEL §§ 843-855.

36. IEL §§ 403-404/645-649; Jacobs § 3.6.

the AFL-CIO in 2007 to come forward with proposals for an Employee Free Choice Act[37] which would give trade unions the possibility to collect members' fees inside the company, once it has reached the 50% plus one of the employees support in the company election. However, this campaign was never successful. It was blocked in the US Congress also during the Obama years, due to the opposition of Republicans and employers.

Now the PRO-Act of the Democrats has the ambition to nullify nationwide the right-to-work laws of the states.

3.3. Collective bargaining

3.3.1. The coverage of collective agreement

As already has been said earlier, the coverage of the American workers by collective agreements is very small: ca. 12% of the working population[38], ca. 7% of private business[39] and ca 37% in the public sector. Most strong is that coverage of the collective agreements, like the rate of union participation in the North-Eastern and most Western States whereas it is weak in most Mid-West and Southern states.[40]

The unions and the Democrats are often blaming this low percentage of collective bargaining to the cumbersome legislation on the duty to bargain and for that reason they have come forward with proposals for a legislative change (see par. 3.3.3). An other factor may also be the low persuading power of the American trade unions. American trade unions have still to learn again to speak the language of the modern worker and to convince them of the blessings of unionisation. In some sections of the trade union movement they have understood this and then a resurrection may be possible. The past few months have seen trade union victories in plants of big American companies were until then there were no recognised unions and collective bargaining: Amazon (New York), Apple (Towson) and Starbucks.

The small coverage by collective agreement does no say that the impact of this small number is as small as that. If in a certain region many workers are under a collective agreement, the standard of the terms and conditions of all workers is levelled up, simply because employers have difficulty in finding qualified personnel prepared to work substantially under the "going rate". But without the cover of a collective agreement the

37. See www.aflcio.org/joinaunion/voiceatwork/efca.

38. ILO Statistics, 2022; (https://www.bls.gov/news.release/union2.t01.htm).

39. IEL § 42; Jacobs § 4.1.

40. IEL § 621; Jacobs § 3.11.

standards are seldom as high as under a collective agreement; estimations range from about 8-25 percent lower.[41] Also the legal guarantees for these standards are much weaker.

3.3.2. The landscape of collective bargaining in the US[42]

Most collective agreements in the US are nowadays concluded between a union and a single company. Sometimes also between several unions and a company, viz. if the company is split up in several distinctive 'bargaining units' (multi-union bargaining).

Only in a few industries there is a sector collective agreement in force (multi-employer bargaining), which is than mostly at local or regional level, but sometimes also at national level.[43]

Most collective agreements continue for a specific number of years.[44] Collective bargaining usually begins a few months prior to the termination of an expiring collective agreement.[45]

3.3.3. The right/duty to 'bargaining in good faith'

The second aim of the NLRA is to protect the right of the employees to bargain collectively through representatives of their own choosing.

As we have seen it is an old habit in the USA that employers do not like trade unions and have done everything to avoid to bargain with them. Nowadays some have come to realise that unions are useful institutions but there are still many employers that prefer to do what they can to avoid collective bargaining with the unions. They often refuse point blank to bargain with a union until the union has demonstrated its majority support. And they will do what they can to prevent a union to gather such a majority support (see 3.2.5.).

For this sake the Federal legislator has developed a quite complicated procedure.

The NRLA (Art. 8(d)) has imposed on employers a 'duty to bargain', a duty to negotiate a collective labour agreement with a trade union. This duty is not a duty to conclude a collective agreement or to do many concessions.

41. IEL §§ 43/368-370.

42. IEL § 43; Jacobs § 4.2.

43. IEL §§ 560-566.

44. IEL § 567/630-634.

45. IEL § 586.

It is only a duty "to meet at reasonable times and confer in good faith".[46]

This obligation should continue until the moment of a "bargaining impasse" is reached. Until that very moment the employer is not allowed to change the existing mandatory conditions of employment. After that moment he may initiate a change in these mandatory conditions of employment if he at least 60 days' prior notice of the intended modifications has given to the other party and at least 30 days prior notice to the Federal Mediation and Conciliation Service and the relevant State mediation agency.[47] As one can imagine there is much debate possible, and therefore there is much case law on the question when this moment of "bargaining impasse" is reached.[48]

It is an unfair labour practice for a union to engage a strike before 60 days have passed after they have served written notice on the employer that they are terminating or modifying the collective agreement or before the expiration date of the contract, whichever is later.[49]

If the parties to the collective negotiation cannot reach an agreement than they may invoke the service of the Federal Mediation and Conciliation Service (3.3.9), but this is voluntary. Only in the health care industry and in national emergency disputes it is obligatory to invoke this service.[50]

3.3.4. The items for collective bargaining

The collective bargaining should be "with respect to wages, hours and other terms and conditions of employment." These are the so-called "mandatory subjects". The parties can of cause also deliberate on other subjects, the "permissive" subjects, as long as they are not "illegal subjects".[51]

The conditions of employment which in Europe are regarded as the normal contents of a collective agreement, are also in the United States the "mandatory subjects" of the collective agreement: wage scales[52], determination of piece rates, incentive pay and profit sharing[53],

46. IEL §§ 569/579; Jacobs § 3.3/4.7.

47. IEL § 574; Jacobs § 4.7.

48. IEL §§ 573-574.

49. IEL § 573/575/580.

50. IEL § 588.

51. IEL §§ 570/655-713; Jacobs, § 4.4.

52. IEL §§ 655-660.

53. IEL § 661.

establishing job classifications, scheduling of working hours[54] and holidays[55], distributing and remuneration of overtime work[56], prescribing safety rules and devices[57], promotion and transfer of employees, dismissals, elaborating personnel policies and shop rules, matters such as sick pay[58] and pensions[59], disciplinary measures[60], seniority[61], training[62] and the peace obligation.[63] Obviously, there is some case law on the fringe.[64]

However, the "duty to bargain" does not reach "managerial decisions which lie at the core of entrepreneurial control". That means that an employer can decide unilaterally to introduce new equipment, close down an operation, eliminate a product, move work to another plant or location, merge with another corporation or sell the business. The same goes for decisions like the selection of managers, declaration of dividends, issuance of new shares, allocation of capital investments.

Unions often try to negotiate provisions on the enterprise's investment decisions, plant closures, sub-contracting of work and changes in production processes, selection and assignment of supervisors, but they seldom are successful in that. It is not forbidden that the parties negotiate on these issues, but it is not covered by the "duty to bargain", so the union cannot force with collective actions the employer to bargain on these matters.[65] The employer also may change these permissive subjects without committing an unfair labour practice.[66] Consequently few employers are willing to include such permissible bargaining subjects in the collective agreement.

If a mandatory subject of bargaining is not resolved by the collective agreement either side may demand changes concerning that subject

54. IEL §§ 662-667.

55. IEL §§ 668-680.

56. IEL §§ 681-685.

57. IEL §§ 712-713.

58. IEL §§ 710-711.

59. IEL §§ 686-693.

60. IEL §§ 694-696.

61. IEL §§ 697-706.

62. IEL § 709.

63. IEL §§ 715-717.

64. IEL §§ 570-572/655-713.

65. IEL § 576.

66. IEL § 576.

during the life of the collective agreement and may bargain about that subject to 'bargaining impasse'. To weaken that right many collective agreements contain a provision, commonly called a 'zipper provision', broadly waiving any further bargaining during the life of the agreement.[67]

With respect to this bargaining in good faith the trade unions are entitled to receive the necessary information about the mandatory subjects, but the courts have read this right to information access narrowly.[68]

3.3.5. Bargaining, but only with the union , that has the support of the majority of the workers in the bargaining unit – if there is one!

However, this entire duty to bargain only applies if a majority of the employees in a "bargaining unit" wants to be represented by a union. Only in that case the employer must recognize and bargain with this union as the "exclusive representative union."

In this context it is a first concern to establish whether there is a union which has effectively the support of 50% + 1 of the workers. This must eventually be shown in elections. And the election must embrace all the workers who would be subjected to a collective agreement. Obviously, all this must occur in a neutral surrounding. Therefore, the NLRA has charged the NLR Board a) to define the 'bargaining unit'[69] and b) to organise and oversee secret elections. On that ballot one of the choices must be: "No Union".

The NLR Board will organise all this as soon as it receives a petition.[70] However, the NLRB operates a so-called 'contract bar rule' which means that if a collective agreement is concluded for a fixed term which is less than three years, it bars the processing of a petition for a representation election challenging the representative status of the majority union which concluded that collective agreement.[71]

As one can easily see all this electoral business has over the years cause a lot of litigation, notably about the boundaries of bargaining units.[72] Trade unions in general like small boundaries, because there the chance of exploiting the solidarity of workers is greatest; employers in general prefer wide boundaries, because there the chance of success for unions

67. IEL § 726/728.

68. IEL § 577; Jacobs § 4.5.

69. IEL §§ 606-628; Jacobs § 3.7.

70. IEL §§ 783-797; Jacobs § 3.7/3.8.

71. IEL §§ 546/568/633; Jacobs 3.10.

72. IEL §§ 606-622; Jacobs § 3.7.

is smaller and it safes them a lot of negotiation time.

Thousands of such elections are held each year and in large number of these elections the employees vote against union representation! One of the reasons for this negative vote is the employers' open opposition to unions. The election is preceded by a campaign period for discussion and debate. Officially the employer is under a duty of neutrality between competing unions.[73] However he may express his feelings about the usefulness of union representation in general. Many employers during this period, will attempt to persuade workers that the union is unnecessary or harmful to their interests. There is a lot of case law on what kind of employers' persuasion is allowed and what not[74] and there are entire law firms specialised in guiding the employers how far they can go. Also, the behaviour of unions in the elections is subject to rules of fair play in the case law of the NLR Board.[75] Failing to comply with these rules, such as recognising a minority union[76], is again an "unfair labour practice".

The PRO-Act, now in the Senate, aims to prevent employers from interfering in union elections and prohibits employers from requiring workers to attend anti-union meetings.

The NLRA does not require that the representative status of a union be established through an NLRB conducted election. As an alternative, an employer can voluntarily recognize a union as bargaining agent for an appropriate bargaining unit if he has a reliable basis for believing that the majority of the employees in the bargaining unit support that union as their bargaining agent. The most common means of providing that proof is in the form of cards signed by the employees authorizing the union to be their bargaining agent. The past two decades have witnessed an upsurge in the number of unions seeking recognition through the use of this card-cheque method.[77] The Democrats would like to give this method a more prominent place in the NRLA and the practice of the NLRB and it is now part of the PRO Act.

So, at the trade union side there can be only one "bargaining agent" (although there may be a plurality of trade unions in a big enterprise with a lot of "bargaining units").

---

73. IEL §§ 425-431.

74. IEL §§ 381-386/389-392; Jacobs § 3.7./3.8.

75. IEL §§ 387-388; Jacobs § 3.7/3.8.

76. IEL §§ 422-424; Jacobs § 3.7.

77. IEL §§ 795.

3.3.6. Application of the collective agreements

When a collective agreement is reached the employer must apply it to all workers of the bargaining unit, both members of the representative unions and non-members. The conditions may not make a differentiation between member and non-members of the union. This is a consequence of the legal duty of fair representation that the majority union has.[78]

The terms and conditions of employment established by the expired collective agreement remain binding until the parties have negotiated to "bargaining impasse."[79]

As has been said before (see par. 2.3) the employer must apply the collective agreement as a standard. He is not allowed to deviate *in peius*, and he is – different from the situation in most European countries – also not allowed to deviate *in melius* - safe when the collective agreement explicitly authorizes that.[80]

3.3.7. Enforcement of the collective agreement

In the cases that trade unions could successfully bargain collective agreements with the employer, the trade union remains involved in its enforcement by the workers' representative at the shop level. Disputes between workers, unions and employers as to the meaning and application of collective agreements are adjudicated by a special system of grievance procedures and arbitration. The grievance procedures are foreseen in the NLRA but they are in concrete laid down in the collective agreement.

Grievance adjudication by arbitration is provided for in most collective agreements but is not mandated by law. Rather, it is based on the parties' agreement. Grievance procedures and arbitration provisions normally apply to all disputes arising out of the collective agreement, but the parties have the power to explicitly exclude particular subjects from the scope of the grievance and arbitration procedures.

Often the first step in a grievance procedure[81] may be initiated by the employee alone, but further processing requires union participation. The next step is an oral presentation by the grievant and his shop steward of the union to the grievant's immediate supervisor. Taking the grievance to higher steps in the process, which is in face of ever higher managerial

78. IEL §§ 540-553.

79. IEL § 633.

80. Jacobs § 4.9.

81. IEL § 719- /825-8.30/Jacobs 11.3.

superiors, normally is the prerogative of the union but some collective agreements allow the worker to initiate appeals to the next step.

The vast majority of disputes are revolved through the grievance process. If, however, the grievance has remained unsettled, there is the arbitration. In most cases a single arbiter will hear the case and issue his opinion and award. The entire procedure takes in average 1,5 year from the moment the case was filed for arbitration. Usually, the parties share equally the arbitrator' fee and expenses.[82]

The NLRA does provide for make whole remedies that include injunctive type relief and in some cases damages in the form of lost pay and benefits or reimbursement of union dues. The Act provides for the payment of fines only in the very narrow situations.

3.3.8. Support for the system of collective agreements

In many European countries there exist a major legislative instrument to promote the coverage of collective agreement: the so-called *erga omnes*-system: The national authorities may declare collective agreement binding for all workers in all companies of a certain sector of industry. If this has occurred all employers in that industry know that their domestic competitors have to pay at least the same wage and other working conditions to their workers. The existence and use of this legal tool is one of the causes that in many European countries collective agreements have a much wider coverage than the rate of organisation of the trade unions can explain.

In the United States such a legislative tool does not exist, neither at state nor at federal level and it is also not on the wish list of the unions.

However, in the USA another legal tool is much used: *contact compliance*. This tool implies that the government – being the federal government, or a state government or a county or municipality – establish the rule that it will only do business with private companies, that have bound themselves on "the prevailing rate" of wages in the region concerned. And that is often more or less the level of a collective agreement.[83]

This tool is helpful to spread the impact of the collective agreement also outside the companies that are legally bound to collective agreements (see 3.3.1). It is on the one hand a forceful tool, because many companies are much dependent of doing business with the governments. On the other hand, it is in several aspects weaker than the *erga omnes* system.

82. IEL §§ 724/881-900.

83. IEL §§ 92/928; Jacobs §§ 9.12/11.8.

First, because all companies which are not interested in doing business with the government are not touched by this tool. Second, because this tool may force the companies to pay more or less the wages contained in the collective agreement, but not other provisions of the collective agreements. Third, because - different from the erga omnes instrument - it gives no direct claim to the workers concerned. Redress against violations requires a very complicated procedure.[84]

3.3.9. Mediation and Conciliation

During the process of collective bargaining, mediators are invited into collective bargaining until when deadlock has arrived or appears imminent.[85] Mediation, however, is voluntary except in the health care industry, in the airline and railway industry or in the occasional situation in which national emergency dispute machinery is invoked. The Federal Mediation and Conciliation Service (FMCS) provides staff specialists to mediate disputes, but sometimes parties retain the service of their own mediator.[86]

Today even when workers succeed in forming a union, nearly half of the newly formed unions fail to ever reach a contract with the employer.

The PRO-Act aims to create a mediation and arbitration process to ensure newly formed unions to reach a first contract. It will impose collective bargaining agreements on employers in the absence of mutual agreement.

3.4. Strikes

3.4.1. Introduction

Strike activity historically was relatively high in the USA as compared with other industrial nations, but it has declined significantly since the early 1980s.[87] Strikes are most frequent in the Eastern and Western States and more rare in most Mid-West and Southern states. Strikes in the US can last for several weeks, and sometimes for month.

3.4.2. The Right to strike

As one could have inferred already from the introductory paragraphs, there is no Right to Strike directly laid down in the American

84. Jacobs § 411/911.

85. IEL § 588.

86. IEL § 588/835-842.

87. IEL §§ 735-736; Jacobs, § 5.1.

Constitution.[88] Some State legislatures and lower courts have sometimes recognized a constitutional right to strike under the due process Clause of the Thirteenth amendment and the speech and assembly clauses of the first Amendment of the American Constitution, but these ideas are not generally shared.[89] Nevertheless, the US Supreme Court has stated that "the presence of economic weapons in reserve and their actual exercise on occasion......is part and parcel of the system that the NLRA/LMRA have recognized."[90]

There is, indeed, a general recognition of the Right to strike in Federal law, viz. in the NLRA/LMRA. Article 7 of the NLRA declares that employees have "a right to engage in concerted activity for collective bargaining and other mutual aid and protection". Strike is defined in this Act as meaning "any concerted stoppage of work, concerted slowdown or other concerted interruption of operations (Art. 501(2) LMRA).[91]

All these concepts are elaborated in the decisions of the NLRB and in the Federal court cases.

The ILO's Committee on Freedom of Association has concluded that several aspects of US law on strikes violates international standards.

3.4.3. General limitations on the right to strike for workers under collective agreements

In the companies that are covered by collective agreement according to the NLRB there are two general limitations on the right to strike in the U.S.: no right to strike during the duration of a collective agreement and not during a 60 days period following a notice of termination of the collective agreement.

When a collective agreement is in force there is no freedom to strike for items in the collective agreement. This because most collective agreements contain a provision to this effect, the so-called peace clauses.[92] Such a provision in a collective agreement does not prohibit a stoppage whose purpose is to protect a significant unfair labour practice nor it will prevent workers for refusing to do abnormally dangerous work (s 502 LMRA).[93]

88. IEL § 735.

89. IEL §§ 451-454.

90. IEL § 583.

91. Jacobs § 5.4.

92. IEL§§ 714/751; Jacobs § 5.6.

93. IEL § 714/754-755; Jacobs § 5.7.

If there has been a collective agreement applicable, before either side may initiate collective action, the start of a concerted action must wait until the end of the period required by the obligation to give a 60 day prior written notice of the intention to terminate or to modify the existing collective agreement and at least 30 days' prior written notice of the labour dispute has been sent to the Federal Mediation and Conciliation Service (art. 8(d) NLRA).[94]

The unions that would organise strikes in violation of these two limitations are guilty of an unfair labour practice.

These two limitations on the right to strike are only applicable on the American workers under a collective agreement. The notice requirements of the NLRA do not apply to employees who are not covered by a collective agreement[95] and obviously also there is no peace clause limiting the right to strike. So, the unions can freely organise strikes for these workers.

If an employer violates a collective agreement that contains a peace provision, the union must seek to resolve its dispute through the grievance-arbitration process. If there is no arbitration provision in the agreement, after taking the matter up with the employer, the union's remedy is to bring suit for breach of contract. The peace provision would be violated if the union were to strike and that strike could be enjoined and the union could be held liable for damages either in arbitration (if the arbitration provision covers the matter) or in court.

Specific limitations on the right to strike[96]

In the companies, which do not fall under a collective agreement not only the unions can organise strikes, also wild-cat strikes are not an unfair labour practice. However, in companies that are under the collective agreement wild cat strikes are unlawful.[97]

In some European states a dogmatic differentiation is made between conflicts of rights and conflicts of interest. Only the last ones are in principle lawful. In the US such a dogmatic difference is not made.[98]

Also different from the situation in some European states, courts in the USA will not apply tests of "proportionality" or "reasonableness" to judge

94. IEL § 582/833-834.

95. IEL § 745.

96. Jacobs, § 5.4.

97. IEL § 747-750; Jacobs § 5.4 .

98. Jacobs § 5.5.

the lawfulness of collective actions.[99] Neither are there obligations on the unions for consultation of the trade union members about taking strike action.[100]

“Slowdowns” and “other concerted interruptions of operations” are included in the definitions of ‘strike” so, basically they may be considered as lawful. Nevertheless there are various cases in which slowdowns, work to rule, a series of short of strikes or “quickie” strikes or intermittent strikes or a refusal to work overtime, a sick-in (workers claim to be too ill to work) have been held by NLRB or the courts to be unprotected.[101] Sit-in strikes are always unlawful, being in violation of the right to property.[102]

Strikes organised by a union for recognition are in principle allowed, but not if there is a collective agreement or a “contract bar” (see 3.3.5) in force. The Act protects an employer from concerted activity in which it is squeezed between the economic pressure exerted by competing labour organisations (the so-called jurisdictional disputes).[103]

Picketing is protected under the Constitutional recognition of free speech/expression as long as it is peaceful. However, posting for the recognition of a trade union is limited.[104] Violent picketing and mass picketing that intimidates or interferes with entering or leaving private property is not protected and can be prosecuted.[105]

Secondary actions (picket lines, sympathy strikes or boycotts) are most of the times not permitted (Art. 8(b)4 NLRA).[106] Even in recent years the US Supreme Court has upheld the strong restrictions on secondary strikes.

The PRO-Act aims at removing prohibitions on workers acting in solidarity with workers at other workplaces & protects workers who engage in peaceful protest actions with their fellow workers.

3.4.4. Position trade unions

A union that organizes an unlawful action against an employer cannot be fined unless it is a penalty imposed for criminal conduct such as violence. In the latter situation, incarceration is also a possibility. However, a

99. Jacobs § 5.8.

100.Jacobs § 5.9.

101. IEL §§ 761-762; Jacobs § 5.10.

102.IEL § 582.

103.IEL § 486-490.

104.Jacobs § 3.10/5.10.

105.IEL § 456; Jacobs § 5.12.

106.IEL §§ 459-485; Jacobs § 5.10.

union can be sued for damages. If the unlawful action has been enjoined by a court and the injunction is violated, it is a contempt of court. At that point, fines can be imposed by the court and the violators can be incarcerated until they cure their violation.

In the public sector a union that tells federal workers to engage in a work stoppage may lose its certification as their bargaining representative.[107]

3.4.5. Position individual strikers

It is evident that American workers forfeit their wage over the days on strike. Most large American unions maintain a reserve fund to pour out benefits to their members participating in work stoppages. It is feed by the regular allocations to it of a set portion of dues income. Strike benefits are never generous.[108]

The NLRA protects workers when they resort to lawful collective action to pressure the employer into making concessions. They continue to be employees during that action. Any disabilities imposed upon the worker as a result of such concerted activity constitute an unfair labour practice. If a collective action is lawful the participant may not be disadvantaged by the employer.

Strikers do not have this protection if their work stoppage is unlawful, e.g. because the notice requirements have been violated, or is in violation of a no-strike provision in the collective agreement, or because of misconduct of a striker. In those cases, an employer can lawfully discharge or otherwise discipline employees participating in such actions.[109]

3.4.6. Position non-strikers

The Act not only protects the right to strike, but also protects the right to refrain from collective activities (art. 7 NLRA). Thus, it is an unfair labour practise for a union to coerce a worker to join a strike. However, if the worker is a union member, the union may use its internal sanctions to coerce compliance of its members with the policies of the union.[110]

3.4.7. The lock out

A classic weapon of the employers against strikes is the lock-out. The NLRA does not specifically address the question of the legal status of a

107. IEL § 738.

108. IEL § 592; Jacobs § 5.13.

109. IEL §§ 581-582/745/763.

110. IEL §§ 765-767; Jacobs § 5.16.

lockout, but the Supreme Court established that lockouts generally are lawful when used as a respond to collective bargaining demands. However, like on the strike there are several restrictions upon the use of the lockout. For instance, a lockout is an unfair labour practice if it is used as a response to a union's demand for recognition or as a means of purging union supporters from the payroll.

Sometimes the employers, like the unions, have adopted employer strike insurance programs.[111]

3.4.8. The right to replace

In the US the main defence for employers against collective actions is in their right to replace striking workers, recognised by the US Supreme Court in the Mackay case. It has ruled that an employer faced with a strike is permitted to hire workers on a temporary or permanent basis to replace the strikers.

If the worker has been replaced while on strike he normally has a statutory right to reinstatement upon termination of the strike.[112] If the employer unlawfully withholds that right to reinstatement, back pay benefits must be paid to remedy the lost opportunity to work.[113] However, there is an important limitation on this right to reinstatement. The employer is allowed to refuse to reinstate a worker while that worker's job is occupied by a replacement hired when the worker was on strike, provided this refusal concerned all the replaced workers, that were on strike.

This rule is different if the strike was against a substantial unfair labour practice of the employer. In that case the employee is entitled to his job back even if replaced by another worker during the strike.[114]

In the early 1990s the unions unsuccessfully mounted a political effort to aim an amendment of the NLRA in order to reduce the circumstances under which employers can lawfully replace strikers.[115]

The PRO-Act aims to prevent employers from permanently replacing workers who participate in a strike.

111. IEL § 594-595.

112. IEL §§ 581/743.

113. IEL §§ 581/741/743; Jacobs § 5.13.

114. IEL § 739-742; Jacobs § 5.14.

115. IEL § 744.

3.4.9. State law

There is not much space for State law in the American law on strikes, as the NLRA pre-empts States from issuing such kind of State laws.[116] State laws however may flourish in the field of the areas not covered by the NLRA, such as State civil servants (see 3.4.10).

3.4.10. Specific regimes[117]

The NLRA/LMRA is only applicable in the private sector, and even that not for the entire private sector. Special strike rules apply in transport (railways and airways).[118] In the health care industry the written notice that must be given before the strike may begin, is 90 days, and the notice to the FMCS is 60 days in advance. Moreover, there is an obligatory cooperation of the parties with inquiry and mediation.[119]

Federal civil servants are not allowed to strike and such a prohibition also applies for most State civil servants. Even in the 12 States, that permit public employee strikes, procedural restrictions are imposed and the right to strike is not extended to all government workers. Nevertheless, the US have seen such strikes, for instance among teachers, in recent years. And the legal restraints on work stoppages are then apparently ignored or evaded, which is a problem in the US.[120] Even in recent years the US Supreme Court has upheld the flat prohibitions on public employee strikes.

In some sectors which are vital for the health and safety of the country the President of the US may order a longer cooling-off period and an obligatory cooperation of the parties with inquiry and mediation.[121]

3.4.11. Enforcement

The NLRB may intervene in disputes over strikes by cease and desist orders. The Courts may issue "injunctions".[122]

An example how all these restrictions can still hinder American workers to take collective action can be seen in the 2006 strike in the New York public transport. For engaging in a 60 hour strike that shut down the city's

116. IEL § 742.

117. Jacobs § 5.3.

118. Jacobs § 5.18.

119. IEL § 746; Jacobs § 5.17.

120. IEL §§ 584/746/737-738/746; Jacobs § 5.3./5.19.

121. Jacobs § 5.7.

122. IEL §§ 816/824/830; Jacobs § 5.11.

subway and bus system, each individual striker was fined two days' pay for every day on strike. Moreover, the trade union was fined 2,5 million dollars. Refusing to pay that, its president was sent to jail! However, this was under the special regime of for government employees and the fines were levied based on the state law regulating employment relations of government workers.

3.4.12. Inquiry, mediation and arbitration

At federal and state level there are services for inquiry, conciliation and mediation in collective labour conflicts available (see 3.3.9).[123]

3.5. Employee involvement in the enterprise

In many European countries there are, besides the trade unions, works councils created to give workers involvement in company affairs.

In the U.S. there is not such a development.[124] Traditionally employee involvement in American enterprise is only done via the trade unions. The trade unions are the only instrument through which workers may participate in the decisions of the enterprise via the collective bargaining system.[125]

Consequently, if the company is bound by a collective agreement there cannot be alternative bodies of worker involvement in company affairs, unless they are established by a collective agreement. Most of the time unions are not receptive to establishing such committees through collective bargaining because they fear that such participation may become a means of undermining the role of the union.[126] If an employer without the approval of the trade union, would set up a works council he would be guilty of an unfair labour practice![127]

Establishment of a worker committee or joint employer-worker committee in an unorganized workplace is lawful so long as the activities of the committee do not constitute collective bargaining. For example, such a committee can lawfully recommend how to improve health and safety or create better relations with customers or the community.

---

123. Jacobs § 5.20.

124. Jacobs § 2.8.

125. This is expressed in IEL in the title of Part II, Ch.4: Worker Participation in Management, which, for European eyes, should have been: Collective Bargaining. In Europe Worker Participation in Management has an overwhelmingly different meaning.

126. IEL § 733.

127. IEL §§ 412-414.

However, few employers like to do such things voluntarily. And there are no federal laws or State laws to impose such an obligation on them.

The result of this situation is, that the overwhelming majority of the American workers still don't have any workers involvement in the enterprise, neither by trade unions nor by other workers' representative bodies. This is certainly one of the great differences with Europe, were most workers are entitled either to representation by trade unions or by other bodies like works councils.

And in the USA there is certainly no legislation in force that obliges companies to a kind of workers representation in (the composition of) the boardrooms, like in some European countries (in Germany: Mitbestimmung), although some companies have given such rights on a voluntary basis to its personnel.

Employee ownership of the voting shares of common stock in the corporations for which they work is widespread. However, it is rare that this gives the employees the power to influence management decision-making.[128]

Concluding remark:

This text has been rewritten during the summer of 2022 in order to give ample attention to the proposals of the Biden administration to renew American federal labour law. It will depend very much on the outcome of the mid-term elections for Congress, November 2022, whether these proposals will make it to the federal statute book of the USA.

Further reading:

For Dutch-speaking students:

- Antoine Jacobs, Sociale Rechten in Amerika, Lemma, Utrecht, 2002, also on the website of Prof. Jacobs: www.antoinejacobs.com

For other students:

- the monography on the United States in R. Blanpain, The International Encyclopaedia of Labour Laws, Kluwer Law International, 2018.
- A.J. Boling and others, Labour and Employment Compliance in the United States, Kluwer Law International, The Hague, 2020.

128. IEL § 733.